Penguin Education

Penguin Education Specials
Willem van der Eyken

The Impact of Robbins
Expansion in Higher Education
Richard Layard, John King and Claus Moser

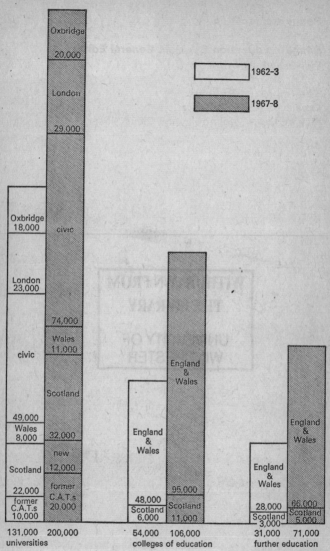

Legend:
- 1962–3 (white)
- 1967–8 (shaded)

universities

131,000 (1962–3):
- Oxbridge 18,000
- London 23,000
- civic 49,000
- Wales 8,000
- Scotland 22,000
- former C.A.T.s 10,000

200,000 (1967–8):
- Oxbridge 20,000
- London 29,000
- civic 74,000
- Wales 11,000
- Scotland 32,000
- new 12,000
- former C.A.T.s 20,000

colleges of education

54,000 (1962–3):
- England & Wales 48,000
- Scotland 6,000

106,000 (1967–8):
- England & Wales 95,000
- Scotland 11,000

further education

31,000 (1962–3):
- England & Wales 28,000
- Scotland 3,000

71,000 (1967–8):
- England & Wales 66,000
- Scotland 5,000

Figure 1. A comparison of the number of full-time students receiving higher education, Great Britain

Penguin Education Special

Special

The impact of Robbins

Richard Layard, John King
and Claus Moser

Penguin Books

Penguin Books Ltd, Harmondsworth,
Middlesex, England
Penguin Books Inc., 7110 Ambassador Road,
Baltimore, Md 21207, U.S.A.
Penguin Books Australia Ltd, Ringwood,
Victoria, Australia

First published 1969
Copyright © London School of Economics, 1969

Made and printed in Great Britain by
Hazell Watson & Viney Ltd, Aylesbury, Bucks
Set in Monotype Times Roman

To
Lord Robbins
with admiration and gratitude

This book is the result of a study carried out in the Higher
Education Research Unit of the London School
of Economics and Political Science.

Contents

Preface

I should like to say a word about the background of this book. One of the effects of the *Robbins Report* was the stimulus it gave to research on higher education. Among the new research enterprises that followed was the Higher Education Research Unit. It had seemed to Richard Layard and myself – who had worked together on the statistical research for the Committee – that there was great scope for enlarging on this kind of work within a university setting, and so we started the Unit in 1964. It was not our intention simply to continue the Robbins projections, since this is the job of government, but when four years had elapsed we felt that the time was ripe for a 'post mortem' on them and on some of the relevant events since Robbins. We were fortunate in being joined by John King, formerly a graduate student of mine, and the book was planned and begun by the three of us. A few months later I went into Whitehall, and the book in its final form is predominantly the work of Richard Layard, helped by John King. The occasion of its publication gives me an appropriate opportunity to express my own admiring appreciation of all Richard Layard did in the research work for the Robbins Committee, and of the various studies he has subsequently conducted or helped on within our L.S.E. Unit.

Claus Moser

Acknowledgements

We are deeply grateful to Miss J. A. Pinney, Research Secretary of the Unit, who has helped us in countless ways throughout the study organizing our drafts and keeping us going with her enthusiasm. We should also like to thank Miss A. Murray and Miss J. Roberts for their help with computing, and Mrs B. Jory for her first-class typing.

In writing the book we have received invaluable help from the members of the Statistics Division of the Planning Branch of the Department of Education and Science. We should like to thank them all for their continual willingness to provide and elucidate data and in particular to express our gratitude to Mr P. Redfern, the Director of Statistics. We have also been greatly helped by the University Grants Committee, the Scottish Education Department, the Universities Central Council on Admissions and many other bodies. We are most grateful to all their statisticians who helped us.

A previous, and more heavily statistical, draft of the book was read by Mr P. Armitage, Dr B. Benjamin, Mr T. Burgess, Dr I. C. R. Byatt, Mr A. A. Croxford, Mr H. L. Elvin, Professor D. L. Foley, Mr H. Glennerster, Mr G. M. Goatman, Mr D. A. C. Heigham, Professor W. R. Niblett, Dr C. M. Phillips, Mr P. Redfern, Mr G. L. Williams, Mr M. V. Wilde and Miss M. Woodhall. We much appreciated their comments. We should also like to thank the staff of Penguin Education, and Mr W. van der Eyken, general editor of the Education Specials, who suggested that the book should appear in that series and made many helpful comments. The study has been financed by the Ford Foundation and we are most grateful for their support.

Chapter One
An Overall View

Apart from electronics and natural gas, higher education has grown faster than any major national enterprise in the 1960s. It is bound to occupy a prominent place in the social histories of the period. From 1962–3 to 1967–8 the number of students in full-time higher education in Britain grew from 217,000 to 376,000, and the increase over these five years was greater than over the preceding twenty-five. An impression of the accelerating pace of change can be seen in Figure 2. The universities grew

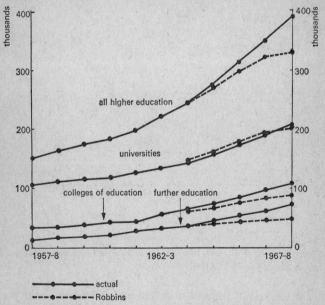

Figure 2. Growth in the actual number of full-time students receiving higher education, compared with growth recommended in the Robbins Report, *Great Britain*

rapidly and were much in the public eye, but in fact the colleges of education and the colleges of 'further education' (technical colleges and the like) grew much faster, and their numbers of students more than doubled in the period.[1]

How has this fantastic explosion come about? And in what sense does it mean that opportunities for people to get into higher education have really improved? Like so many things, this question is best looked at in terms of demand and supply. The number of students depends on how many people want to study, and on how many places are provided.

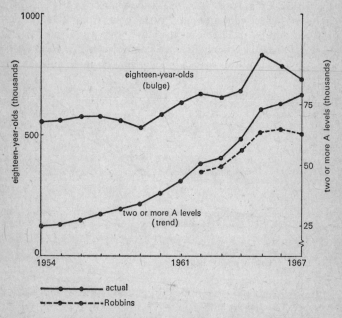

Figure 3. Number of eighteen-year-olds in June and number obtaining two or more A levels, England and Wales

On the side of demand, two forces have been at work: the 'bulge' and the 'trend'. The bulge is the increased number of children born in the middle of the Second World War and, especially, just after it ended. Its result, as can be seen in Figure 3, is a massive inflation in the number of eighteen-year-olds in the early 1960s. In June 1965, for example, there were nearly a quarter more people aged eighteen than there were twelve months earlier.

Of itself, this would have enormously increased the demand for higher education. But on top of the bulge was superimposed the 'trend', that is the increase in the proportion of people of a given age who get good school-leaving qualifications, many of whom will seek higher education. This trend, shown in Figure 4,

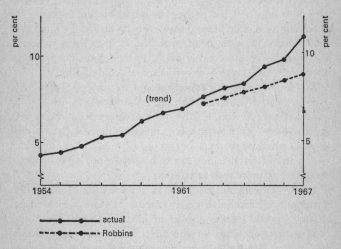

Figure 4. *The percentage of the age group obtaining two or more A levels, England and Wales*

was a well-established phenomenon long before the bulge reached the school leaving age. But it has actually become accentuated as the bulge has passed through the sixth forms – a considerable tribute to those responsible for putting roofs over the extra heads, and teachers in front of their desks. Thus in 1955 under one in twenty of the young people of the country were getting two or more Advanced levels in the General Certificate of Education. This figure of 4·5 per cent had risen to 6·9 per cent by 1961 – an addition of 2·4 per cent in six years. But by

1967 the proportion was no less than 10·9 per cent – over one in ten; and the addition over these six years was 4·0 per cent, a definite upturn on the earlier trend.

What accounts for these trends? It is impossible to answer this precisely. Doubtless a basic underlying cause is general economic growth. But why exactly does this raise the demand for education? People seek education both for its own sake as a form of 'consumption', and as an 'investment' providing the means to a higher income. As a good in itself, education is felt to add to the interest and grace of life; and when people get richer they seek more of it, just as they buy more novels or hi-fi sets. The education of a child places heavy costs on his family in terms of loss of earnings, even if tuition is free. And, as living standards rise, people can more easily afford to meet these costs, just as they can afford more of other forms of 'consumption'.

But people also want education as a way to better-paid jobs. And as a country grows richer, the labour market's demand for educated people rises relative to the demand for those with lesser skills – much of modern capital equipment can only be used by educated workers and so on. As a result the number of people for whom education can be financially profitable increases steadily, and more seek to be educated.

But growing national income is not the only cause of this. There are other important social factors at work, which do not depend directly on the growth of income. These factors may tend to raise the place of education in the scale of individual preferences. Perhaps the most important of them is the educational level of parents, which is known to have a potent effect on the educational aspirations and achievements of their children. In this way higher education tends to spread like an infectious disease, multiplying itself from generation to generation. Similarly, the more educated people there are in the community, the easier it is for young people to acquire information about education. Thus the growing public debate about higher education, in the press, radio and television, through parent–teacher associations and in Parliament, depends on a more or less educated public. In turn it informs growing numbers of young people, and their parents, about the opportunities in a higher education system which might otherwise remain incomprehensible and awesome. Likewise, the spread of higher education tends to make possession of a higher qualification a more and more indispensable symbol of status. In these various ways, higher education resembles a snowball steadily growing by virtue of its own momentum. However, the resources of individual families and of public authorities impose limits on this process, and higher education's unparalleled growth since the Second World War has happened largely because of the unprecedented rate of economic growth over the period.

In any case, the A level trend, however caused, together with the bulge has produced an increase in the number of people with good school-leaving qualifications that is truly astonishing. The result is shown in Figure 3. We do not have very reliable data on how many of these people have applied to higher education, but it seems that the proportion of people at each level of qualification who apply for full-time education has been fairly stable. Their applications constitute the demand for places.

What of the supply? In a centralized educational system like our own, or even more, say, the French, the supply is basically controlled by the central government – which is not at all the case in, for example, North America. So the answer amounts to a description of how the government has reacted. During the 1950s the government did not have any concerted plan for higher education as a whole. Responsibility for the different parts was divided. The universities got their money from the Treasury through the University Grants Committee (U.G.C.), and the U.G.C. did most of what thinking there was on future expansion. The quinquennial settlement of the U.G.C. recurrent grant was normally based on a target number of places, arrived at by extrapolating trends in staying on at school and assuming that the average quality of those staying on was likely to fall. The rest of higher education in England and Wales came under the Ministry of Education, but there was little co-ordination between the planning of the teacher training colleges and the area known as 'further education'. Teacher training was, and still is, planned in relation to the country's needs for teachers – and rightly so. Further education was not in general planned in any quantitative sense. Ten colleges of advanced technology (C.A.T.s) had, it is true, been selected for special treatment and were the subject of definite plans. But the rest of the colleges – polytechnics, technical colleges, art colleges and so on – were rapidly developing their full-time work as a result of local initiative and increased demand for places, without any clear overall strategy.

These fluid and unco-ordinated arrangements for the management of higher education might have survived, had it not been for the pressure of expanding demand. This had a number of effects. First, the output of school leavers with at least the minimum university entrance qualifications (two A levels), grew much faster than the number getting in to university. As a result the proportion of people with these qualifications who went to university fell from nearly 80 per cent in 1956 to 65 per cent in 1961.[2] The story is illustrated in Figures 5 and 6, and in Table 1. It prompted a chorus of complaints at the increasing difficulties of university entry. In addition there was the menace of the approaching bulge, which again raised fundamental

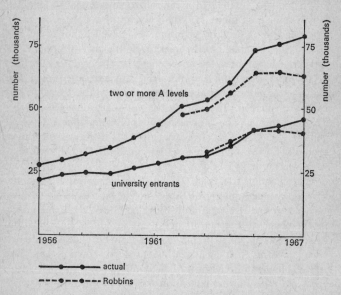

Figure 5.   Number obtaining two or more A levels and number entering university from England and Wales

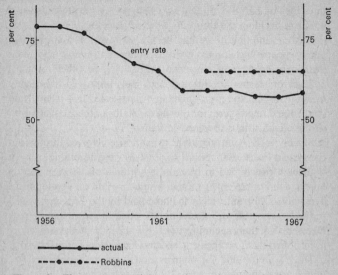

Figure 6. The percentage of those with two or more A levels entering university from England and Wales

Table 1

Number obtaining Two or More A Levels and Number Entering Full-time Higher Education from England and Wales

	Numbers obtaining 2 or more A levels	University entrants (including former C.A.T.s)	All entrants	University entrants as % of those with 2 or more A levels	All entrants as % of those with 2 or more A levels
1956	27,000	21,000	36,000	79	133
1961	43,000	28,000	52,000	65	120
1962	51,000	30,000	57,000	59	112
1963	53,000	32,000	64,000	59	121
1964	61,000	36,000	74,000	59	121
1965	73,000	42,000	87,000	57	119
1966	75,000	43,000	95,000	57	126
1967	79,000	46,000	104,000	58	131

questions about the principles which the government should adopt in deciding the future number of places.

At the same time there had been a spillover of well-qualified young people no longer able to go to university who went instead to colleges of advanced technology, or other technical colleges or teacher training colleges. This improved the quality of students in the non-university parts of the system, and contributed to pressures for raising the status of these colleges and of the qualifications obtained in them.

Moreover, the sums of public expenditure involved throughout the system (over £200 million by 1962–3) were becoming so large that there clearly had to be more co-ordination between sectors and a definite rationale to the whole process of development. The university grant was at the time paid by the Treasury, which normally controls the spending of other government departments rather than spending itself. As the size of the university grant grew, this arrangement became increasingly embarrassing.

These were among the main reasons why the Robbins Committee was appointed in early 1961.[3] It was asked:

to review the pattern of full-time higher education in Great Britain and in the light of national needs and resources to advise Her Majesty's Government on what principles its long-term development should be based. In particular, to advise, in the light of these principles, whether there should be any changes in that pattern, whether any new types of institution are desirable and whether any modifications should be made in the present arrangements for planning and co-ordinating the development of the various types of institution.

This was a very wide remit, and the Committee's Report, not to mention its appendixes which weighed seven pounds, covered almost every aspect of higher education one might care to mention – except student protest, which was then non-existent. Our book is not about every aspect of higher education.[4] It is about expansion – its scale and pattern, its implications for educational opportunity, and the means by which it has been achieved, with a brief glance at the future. As education is a seamless robe, we shall nevertheless refer to many of the main events in higher education; but the focus is on expansion.

The *Robbins Report* provided an explicit philosophy of expansion and a detailed plan embodying it,[5] including a five-year crash programme up to 1967–8 to deal with the bulge. In this book we are asking: how has the plan worked out? Or to put it another way round: what difference has Robbins made?

The Robbins Committee's golden rule for the supply of places was that: 'courses of higher education should be available for all those who are qualified by ability and attainment to pursue them and who wish to do so'. Thus they sided with those who argued that the supply of places should be based on the demand for places from potential entrants, rather than on the demand in the economy for the products of higher education. The statistical problem was to translate this general exhortation into an operational rule. The rule adopted was that the proportions of people with each level of entry qualification who actually go to higher education should remain constant (at their 1961 proportions) up to 1968, and then rise somewhat. Entrants to higher education have a variety of qualifications, but the method meant in effect assuming that the number of entrants should continue to equal roughly 120 per cent of the output of people with two or more A levels, as it had in 1961 (see Table 1). This may seem a strange procedure until one reflects that there are many entrants with less than two or more A levels; conversely it does not of course imply that all people with two or more A levels go to higher education.

A similar rule was laid down for universities – the number of entrants should continue at 65 per cent of the output of those with two or more A levels. In this way the proportion of entrants to higher education who went to university would remain stable at just over a half.

The mechanics of the plan were thus:

1. Forecast the A level output.
2. Multiply this by the proportions above to obtain numbers of entrants.
3. Assume certain lengths of course to convert entrants to places for home students.
4. Add in overseas students.
5. Calculate needs for staff and finance.

Step 1 required a prediction, but all the other steps required value judgements about ratios and led to prescriptions about numbers.

In chapter 3 we shall conduct a post mortem on the A level prediction made by the Committee, and in chapters 4 to 9 on the pattern of expansion in the universities and in the other parts of higher education. Chapter 10 will show what staff and money have been forthcoming, and chapter 11 will look to the future. The book is not however only about numbers and chapter 2, which deals with the public debate about expansion, includes no figures at all.

But first we must go back to our original question. How *has* the government reacted? Few official reports in British history, and certainly in educational history, have led to such immediate changes in government policy. Many of the qualitative recommendations were, it is true, left in abeyance, but the quantitative recommendations up to 1973–4 were accepted in a White Paper published within 24 hours of the *Report*.[6] The *Report* could not have come out at a better time with a general election in the offing, and this more than snobbery may help to explain why it got a quicker reaction than Crowther and Plowden, both of which came out just after elections. But more important was the imminence of the bulge and the government's genuine belief in the importance of higher education on both social and economic grounds.[7] Not only were the recommendations accepted but they have been carried out in all sectors, with teacher training and further education overshooting their targets by wide margins. The picture is shown in Figure 2 and in Table 2.

But this is not the whole story. For in the meantime the output of A levels has been higher than Robbins predicted – 26 per cent higher by 1967. Yet in the years up to 1967–8, the university provision has not been raised above the Robbins targets – the spillover has again been channelled into the non-university sector.[8] As Table 1 showed, opportunities to enter higher education as a whole have if anything improved, but it has become more difficult to enter university than it was in 1961 – the standard of competition which Robbins recommended maintaining. The Robbins numbers have been maintained, but the Robbins principles let slip. As a result the share of universities in higher education has fallen sharply – from 60 per cent of places in 1962–3 to 53 per cent today (see Table 2). This

Table 2
Students in Full-time Higher Education, Great Britain

| | Number of students (thousands) | | | | | | | | Percentage of students in universities | |
| | Universities (including former C.A.T.s) | | Colleges of education | | Further education | | All full-time higher education | | | |
	Actual	Robbins	Actual	Robbins	Actual	Robbins	Actual	Robbins	Actual	Robbins
1957–8	103	•	33	•	13	•	148	•	69	•
1962–3	131	•	55	•	31	•	217	•	60	•
1963–4	140	142	62	59	36	36	238	238	59	60
1964–5	154	156	71	66	43	39	267	262	57	60
1965–6	169	173	82	74	51	42	302	290	56	60
1966–7	184	187	95	80	59	45	339	312	54	60
1967–8	200	197	106	84	71	47	376	328	53	60
Percentage growth 1962–3 to 1967–8	53	50	93	54	129	51	74	51	•	.

development is in line with the government's 'binary' policy, which aims to build up the non-university sector relative to the universities.

However, the divergence between present government policy and the Robbins approach is far less striking than the difference between pre-Robbins and post-Robbins government policy. As we have mentioned, the policy before Robbins, or the absence of it, had reduced the proportion of those with two or more A levels who entered university from nearly 80 per cent in 1956 to 65 per cent in 1961. In 1962, before Robbins reported, the proportion again fell, to 59 per cent. But the really striking fact is that since then the proportion has not fallen at all – a complete reversal of previous trends.

What does this mean in terms of educational opportunity? In the years before Robbins, the opportunities for 'qualified school leavers' to enter universities were falling, although the number of 'qualified school leavers' was rising only slowly. In the years after, their opportunities remained constant, although their

Table 3

Home Entrants to Full-time Higher Education as Percentage of the Age Group, from England and Wales

	Universities (including former C.A.T.s)	Colleges of education	Further education	All higher education
1956	3·8	2·2	0·4	6·4
1957	4·2	2·3	0·5	7·0
1958	4·4	2·5	0·7	7·7
1959	4·4	2·8	0·8	8·0
1960	4·4	2·8	1·0	8·2
1961	4·5	2·6	1·2	8·3
1962	4·5	2·6	1·4	8·5
1963	4·7	3·1	1·7	9·5
1964	4·9	3·3	1·8	10·0
1965	5·3	3·7	2·0	11·0
1966	5·5	4·2	2·3	12·0
1967	6·3	4·8	3·2	14·3

number was exploding. Or if we look at opportunities in relation to the whole population of the relevant age, the proportion of young people going to university had been static from 1958 to 1962 at around 4·5 per cent; in the five years after that it rose to 6·3 per cent. This is shown in Table 3. And the proportion going to all forms of higher education, which had also been fairly stagnant, rose from 8·5 per cent to 14·3 per cent. This is the measure of the impact of Robbins.

Chapter Two
The Debate about Expansion

The government accepted the Committee's plan, but how did the public react? If sales are the index, the *Robbins Report* was a *succès fou*: the only official reports to have sold more copies are Beveridge on social insurance and Denning on Christine Keeler. But how did people take to the Committee's approach to expansion?

The majority supported it but at the same time a lively debate was joined on three main issues which are still as relevant as they were then. The first is the question of the pool of untapped ability and its size. When the Committee was set up there was probably a majority of educated opinion which thought there was some limit, that would soon be approached, in the proportion of people who could benefit from higher education. But the very setting up of a Committee, and the debate which follows, often completely changes the whole climate of public opinion about the issue being investigated. This is certainly what happened with Robbins. During the two-and-a-half years of the Committee's work, the 'limited pool of ability' school of thought was in progressive retreat. The Committee's foreign visits drew attention to the lengths to which things seemed to have gone in other countries without loss of quality; and when the *Robbins Report* was published the Committee's survey results further strengthened the hands of those who believed in the importance of environment in determining intellectual attainment. Thus, by 1963, it seemed much more widely acceptable to look forward to an endless upward trend in higher education in the foreseeable future, and not, as had been customary, to look for a plateau.

Of the major newspapers, only *The Times* was noticeably hostile to the philosophy of 'More will not mean worse'; and, although chided by Sir Geoffrey Crowther for intellectual 'Bourbonism'[1] its hostility did not diminish with time. A part of the trouble was based on a misunderstanding of the term 'qualified school leavers', which had occupied a fundamental place in the Robbins recommendations. This term had been used in the *Report* in an entirely neutral sense to mean those holding particular qualifications (e.g. two or more A levels), and not in a prescriptive sense to mean that everyone with such qualifications was fit to have a place. *The Times* in its leaders implied that Robbins had said that all with two or more A levels should go to university if they wanted. This point was ultimately clarified.[2]

Other critics questioned the appropriateness of numbers obtaining G.C.E. as the basis from which to deduce numbers suitable for higher education, and they implied that this method somehow overestimated future requirements. This criticism assumes that past trends in G.C.E. have not corresponded to trends in numbers suitable for higher education. In fact we believe these two trends have been broadly similar. This was the reason for the claim in the *Robbins Report*[3] that what is being projected *is* a number proportional to those suitable for higher education, and that for convenience only we label this number by familiar qualifications. The method would not be invalidated even if G.C.E. were abolished.

An annual signal for the 'limited pool of ability' school to show itself has been the publication of the figures of vacancies in university departments. It is true that these vacancies, which are almost entirely in science and technology, raise important issues of the balance between faculties, but they normally represent not more than one or two per cent of all places. Moreover, the annual expansion in student numbers is always many times the number of vacancies in the previous year. Though frictional under-utilization of capacity should be cut to the minimum, it is hardly a sign that the general philosophy of expansion is wrong. There is no overall shortage of well-qualified applicants, though there is an imbalance between faculties. In any case, the whole concept of a vacancy is ambiguous since the number of places an institution is willing to offer depends in part on the applicants expected.

A second and more fundamental criticism of the *Report* attacked the whole philosophy of basing provision in higher education on the demand of school leavers for places. From one side it was urged that the pool of untapped ability is so large that plans for higher education should not involve a passive response to the increasing numbers of able people coming forward; but should rather be geared to plans for positively mobilizing mute inglorious Miltons whose talents still go to waste.[4] It is easy to sympathize with this point of view, especially when there is in Britain such an irrational dearth of sixth-form maintenance grants relative to the scale of grants for higher education. However, there is a real difficulty in this approach. How much talent should be mobilized? It is difficult to decide this without bringing in some other planning criterion as well. We shall never be able to educate all men and women to the limits of their ability, because this phrase has no meaning: there is no environment so favourable that, in a better one, people will not be able to learn more. So what other criterion can we invoke?

The one most commonly urged by the critics of Robbins is, of course, the manpower criterion. Higher education should be geared not to the demand for places but to the demand for higher-educated people in the economy. The *Robbins Report* rejected this latter basis, except for teacher training, both because of their desire to meet the 'social' demand from boys and girls, and because of their doubts about the possibilities of accurate estimates of manpower needs.

Estimating these needs is certainly very difficult, but it seems inevitable and desirable that it should in the long run come to play a bigger role in educational planning than it could in the *Robbins Report*. In public services, like education and medicine, it is easier to assess needs than in the private sector, since the state is the sole employer and can, if it wants, decide in advance how many people it is going to employ. As a result the best forecasting work in Britain has been on teacher needs; needs for doctors have also been studied, less successfully. On private sector employees the main research effort has been directed at scientists and engineers. Here, as in principle with all manpower forecasts, there are two main difficulties: first of deciding to what extent present demand is being appropriately met, and second of forecasting future shifts in demand. In Britain, research has been concerned chiefly with forecasting changes in demand, using either employers' forecasts for fairly simple relationships between output levels and highly qualified manpower.[5] Research on manpower forecasting is continually helping to improve these methods and it is very important from the point of view of educational planning, that it should be energetically pursued in the academic world and in government. At the same time, we need to learn more about the extent to which the present manpower position is optimal. In this, rate of return analysis has a role to play. A starting point, on which it would be relatively simple to agree, is that an optimal situation is one where the marginal benefits per unit of cost are neither greater nor less in higher education than in any other sphere of national activity. But the difficulty comes in measuring benefits. The increased productivity of those with higher education can be measured roughly by how much more they are paid than people without higher education, but in addition one man's education may have important effects on the productivity of others and this must be allowed for. On the manpower criterion productivity is all we take into account, but we can, if we like, take a wider view and add in something for the value of higher education for its own sake. When these benefits are expressed as a proportion of cost, we have an estimate of the social rate of return on higher education. A good deal of work is proceeding on this front, but, largely for lack of data, neither this kind of rate of return analysis nor forecasts of shifting demand have yet reached the point where they can be used directly to obtain estimates of future student numbers needed in Britain.

However, there is of course a close link between the growth in the numbers who would be justified on social rate of return grounds, and in the numbers which would arise on the Robbins criteria of demand for places. For the private demand for places depends, amongst other things, on the private rate of return to be got from undertaking higher education, while the number of places justified on social cost-benefit grounds depends on the social rate of return. On some quite plausible assumptions these two rates of return will move in step;[6] thus private demand will only surge forward when people with higher education can be productively employed and vice versa. One key assumption, however, is the continuation of present policies on subsidies to students. The Robbins Committee judged that, given prevailing attitudes to education, these ought to be maintained for a time, on social grounds. It is clear however that if the private price were raised, the private demand would be lower than otherwise. The Robbins Committee have been wrongly charged with being unaware of the fact.[7]

A third major line of criticism came from those who thought that, though there might be enough suitable students worth educating, there would not be enough staff. The *Report* contained the tautological statement that on certain assumptions a system expanding at a constant or declining rate of compound interest could staff itself. This was admitted to be true, but critics argued that the steady state assumption was irrelevant and that short-run problems were formidable.[8] Calculations in the *Robbins Report* had in fact explicitly pointed to these short-run problems. But events have on the whole disproved the fears; and, though the average quality of teachers may have fallen, staff/student ratios have not. At the same time teachers' salaries kept pace in general with other salaries up till near the end of the crisis period. Though the climate in higher education is chillier nowadays, it is a fact that the expansion programme in the bulge years succeeded because the government not only willed the end but willed the means.

Chapter Three
The Upsurge at A Level

It is time to trace the story in more detail. We need to begin in the schools, where the pressures for expansion are generated. As we showed in Figure 3, the Robbins forecast of the A level trends was too low. By 1967 the number of people getting two or more A levels had risen to 79,000 compared with 63,000 predicted by Robbins – a difference of about 26 per cent, only six years after the base year from which the forecast was made.[1] How did this come about?

To a limited extent it was deliberate. The Robbins Committee believed that the best way to get their expansion plan accepted was to base it on assumptions so modest that no reasonable man could reject them. They therefore explicitly took an A level projection representing a minimum of what they thought was likely.[2] But even a bolder forecast would probably have been surpassed by what has in fact happened.

The bulge was of course predictable, and accurately so – the number of eighteen-year-olds can be forecast more or less right for up to eighteen years ahead. The problem was the trend. Robbins predicted that the proportion of the age group obtaining two or more A levels would rise from 6·9 per cent in 1961 to 8·8 per cent in 1967. In fact, as Table 4 shows, it rose to 10·9 per cent. Thus the actual increase over the six years was 4·0 per cent of the age group – an average of over 0·6 per cent a year, compared with a forecast of 0·3 per cent. These figures are shown in Table 5 together with the comparable figures for the earlier years.

The really striking point is that in the earlier years the average increase was under 0·4 per cent. Thus the 1960s have seen a sharp upswing in the tendency to get A levels. The upswing has been much greater for girls than boys, and the error in the Robbins prediction was greater for girls than boys. In fact from 1961

Table 4

Percentage of the Age Group Obtaining Two or More A Levels and Staying at School Aged Seventeen, England and Wales

	1954	1961	1967 Actual	1967 Robbins
Obtaining two or more A levels				
Boys	5·7	8·7	13·0	*11·2*
Girls	2·9	5·1	8·6	*6·3*
Boys and girls	4·3	6·9	10·9	*8·8*
At school, aged seventeen				
Boys	8·6	13·1	17·4	*16·8*
Girls	7·1	10·2	14·6	*12·6*
Boys and girls	7·9	11·7	16·0	*14·8*

Table 5

Average Annual Increment in the Percentage of the Age Group obtaining Two or More A Levels and Staying at School Aged Seventeen, England and Wales[4]

	1954–61	1961–7 Actual	1961–7 Robbins
Obtaining two or more A levels			
Boys	0·43	0·72	*0·42*
Girls	0·31	0·58	*0·21*
Boys and girls	0·37	0·67	*0·31*
At school, aged seventeen			
Boys	0·65	0·72	*0·64*
Girls	0·44	0·75	*0·41*
Boys and girls	0·54	0·74	*0·53*

Winchester University Libraries

Self Service Receipt for Borrowed Items

Name: ****1622

Title: 04194438

Item: 04194438

Due Back: Item does not exist

Title: Fifty key sociologists.

Item: 03866564

Due Back: 23/07/2022 18:00:00

Title: Being a university /

Item: 03995909

Due Back: 23/07/2022 18:00:00

Title: The impact of Robbins /

Item: 00624683

Due Back: 23/07/2022 18:00:00

Total Borrowed: 3
25/06/2022 14:02:25

Thank you for using self service.

Mike Shattock
CE7003

to 1967 the average annual increment in proportions with A levels was almost as high for girls as for boys. And if we express the increment as a percentage rate of growth (on the 1961 base) it is much higher – an 11 per cent rate of growth for girls compared with 8 per cent for boys.[3] Bit by bit the sex gap is closing.

What explains the all-round accentuation of the A level trend in this decade? Unfortunately we cannot say much about the underlying causes. The *Robbins Report* spelt out in some detail the kinds of factors which affect school performance and the demand for higher education.[5] As we suggested in Chapter one, these are essentially: the employment prospects for those who stay on, which represent the monetary benefits from doing so; the financial terms on which education is available, which affect the costs; parental income, which determines the ability to finance a period of study and also influences the 'consumption' demand for education; and a whole host of social factors which affect the values attached to education.

Many 'cross-sectional' studies, comparing individuals at a particular point in time, have estimated the effect on school performance of such factors as family income, parental education and individual ability.[6] But these studies do not take into account the effect of influences such as employment prospects or the level of grants, which vary over time in ways that affect all members of the community. What one is really looking for is a quantitative explanation of trends over time in the demand for education.[7] One approach is to look at the relation of education and Gross National Product, but in this there is, of course, the difficulty of determining whether growing G.N.P. promotes staying on through its effect on employment prospects or by stimulating the demand for education 'for its own sake'. From a forecasting point of view, however, this problem is not crucial, and it therefore seemed worthwhile to look at the possibility of using short-run movements of the economy as a guide in short-run educational forecasting. However, the tabulation of annual growth of A levels, and of staying on at school, against changes in real national income show no convincing links between them.[8]

In the present state of our knowledge of these complex

relationships, we thus end up treating the trends in education as if they depend on the passage of time, rather than on the variables which really produce them. But even this simple approach raises difficulties, in particular the technical problem of the shape of the underlying time series. There is unlikely in principle to be any simple expression which adequately describes these trends, since, being the product of a complex of variables their relationship with time is likely to be changing. However, there are two simple models that may be considered: simple interest growth or compound interest growth. The former corresponds to a straight line trend, the addition each year being the same. The latter corresponds to an exponential trend, in which the increment each year is not the same, but grows over time.

We said earlier that the average annual increment in the proportions obtaining A levels has grown. This would seem to suggest compound rather than simple interest growth. But

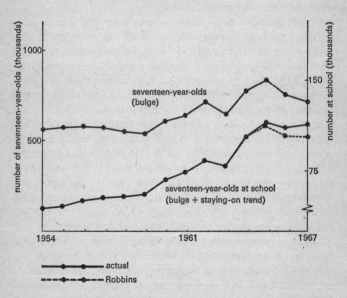

Figure 7.   Number of seventeen-year-olds in January and number of them at school, England and Wales

unfortunately, if we make the compound interest assumption, we find that the rates of growth have been falling with time, rather than being constant. Official forecasts are still essentially based on the straight-line approach. Further research might lead to a more satisfactory formulation than either of the obvious contending approaches, but is limited by the small number of years for which data are available.[9]

We can, however, use plain arithmetic to discover a number of interesting facts about the trends. In doing so, we shall break down the numbers getting A levels into two components: first, the numbers who stay on at school to different ages; and, second, the proportion of these stayers-on who obtain A levels. This was the approach used in the Robbins forecasts.

First comes staying on. Here the forecast has been relatively accurate. Its assumption was that the proportion staying on would grow in the same straight line as in the past, as shown in Figure 8. Broadly speaking this is what has happened, with the exception of the year 1967.

This illustrates a remarkable fact about the British and many other educational systems. Suppose we want to predict the numbers of seventeen-year-olds at school. The simplest way would be to project the past trends in the absolute numbers, but in this particular period this would have produced hopelessly wrong results. This can be seen in Figure 7. If the reader uses a ruler to extrapolate the trend in numbers of seventeen-year-olds at school over the period of 1954–61, he will find himself predicting about 100,000 in 1967. He would thus have been about 15,000 too low and even further out in 1965. The reason is of course the demographic fluctuations of the period. But what is suprising is that, if we take these fluctuations into account, the proportion of young people staying on shows such an uncannily stable trend, much stabler for example than the trend in G.N.P.[10] The mechanism whereby this comes about must be complicated. It seems to imply that in any particular year the pattern of attainments in an age cohort is independent of its size, and that it is this pattern that determines, through its effect on attitudes of school teachers, parents and children, the proportion who stay on. Even so, it seems odd that the absolute number is more or less irrelevant, considering that it is the absolute number who have to be provided with desks and teachers and the absolute number who have to find suitable jobs. This also has implications for the economic interpretation of the demand for education. For, if an unusually large number of children suddenly seek higher education, presumably the job opportunities for each stayer-on are less favourable than they would normally be. But this does

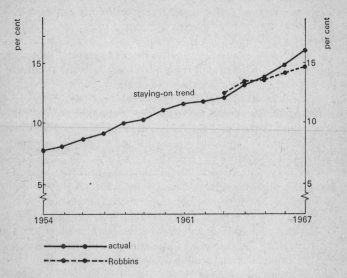

Figure 8.   The percentage of seventeen-year-olds at school in January, England and Wales

not seem to deter larger numbers from staying on, when an unusually large age group happens to come along. There must be something wrong with the theory that individuals do their own manpower forecasting, unless they do it very badly. However, it is still quite likely that prospective students are influenced by the current market situation, while not attempting to forecast how that situation will have changed by the time their own education is completed.[11]

Though the Robbins staying on forecast was fairly successful up to 1966, the A level forecast went wrong. Whereas the

Robbins Committee assumed that the proportions of leavers of each age who obtain a given qualification would remain constant, they have in fact risen. At the time of the *Robbins Report* there was no good evidence on what these various proportions had been over the years. But some evidence suggested that for boys the ratio between the total numbers of A level passes and the numbers staying on had been constant, while it had risen for girls.[12] The Committee therefore thought that the future estimates for girls 'may well prove to be considerable underestimates'.[13]

Table 6

School Leavers with Two or More A Levels as Percentage of Leavers of Each Age, England and Wales

| | *Leavers aged 18* | | *Leavers aged 17* | |
	Boys	*Girls*	*Boys*	*Girls*
1961	66	54	20	14
1962	69	56	23	16
1963	70	60	20	14
1964	69	60	23	18
1965	71	61	24	17
1966	71	62	26	18
1967	72	62	29	19

As Table 6 shows, this hunch was right. For girls leaving at seventeen and eighteen – the majority of those who have A levels leave at these ages and especially at eighteen – the proportions having each number of A level passes (one or more, two or more and three or more) have all risen, and in many cases considerably. The same is true of boys, though among the eighteen-year-olds the increases are less.

This finding is contrary to many commonly accepted dogmas. At the extreme is the *a priori* view that, as more people stay on at school, they are bound to do worse – 'More *means* worse'. But there is also the common view that as a matter of fact the 'new' kind of stayer-on is increasingly not taking A levels, but rather some form of pre-vocational course or delayed O levels. Again, untrue – so far. The proportions of eighteen-year-old leavers who had attempted one or more A levels rose between 1962 and 1967 – for boys from 92 to 95 per cent, and for girls from 87 to 92 per cent. At the same time A level pass rates for boys and girls remained generally stable over the period. So the increased proportions obtaining A levels seem to be mainly the result of increased proportions attempting them.

This process clearly cannot go on for ever, as the proportions cannot exceed 100 per cent. Moreover general comprehensive schooling will certainly encourage the growth of non-A-level courses in the sixth form. But this only raises another question: what will comprehensive schooling do to the staying-on trend in schools? We expect it to increase the annual increment in staying on, and at the same time to decrease the proportions of stayers-on who get A levels. This example illustrates a statistical problem of some importance: is it best to make separate projections for the two stages mentioned – first 'staying on' and then the proportion of stayers-on who qualify – or would a more accurate answer be obtained by directly projecting the proportions of the age group obtaining A level? We prefer the latter approach, as there is strong evidence that in years when unusually large numbers stay on they do unusually badly and vice versa. As a statistical test we have used the available data for 1961–6 to predict in retrospect the A level results in those years, using the two-stage and one-stage method; the error of prediction was smaller using the one-stage approach.[14]

This issue is not altogether academic, as the projections which emerge are used to make plans which determine the futures of many young people. The present method tends naturally to produce forecasts implying smaller future increments in the proportions with A level than have occurred in the past. This is because of the 100 per cent limit we have mentioned. It can be seen from Table 5, that a simple extrapolation of the proportions of the age group with A levels would have led to a better prediction, than the two-stage method actually used by Robbins. The same policy might well lead to better forecasts now, if it were adopted, but we shall leave to the last

chapter our look at the current projections made for the government.

Enough of the niceties of forecasting trends in the schools.
There remains the question of those who get A levels in technical
colleges. In progressive circles it is common to talk as though
young people are now so averse to life at school that the technical
colleges are becoming the main route to A levels. This is quite
wrong, and even now the colleges only account for 10 per cent of
A level passes. However, the numbers of A levels in technical
colleges has grown very rapidly, and the Robbins forecast was
outdistanced more here than in any other sector. Robbins
predicted that in 1967 there would be 3,800 home students
obtaining two or more A levels in further education: the actual
output was 7,700 (5,200 men and 2,500 women).[15] The Robbins
method was a straight line extrapolation of numbers, which as
we have already pointed out, is likely to be extremely in error
when demographic fluctuations are sharp. The method now
adopted by the Department of Education and Science is to
relate A levels in technical colleges to the number of school
leavers with 'five or more O levels but no A levels' three years
earlier, and to project the rising trend in this ratio. In 1961 the
ratios for those with two or more A levels were 12 per cent for
boys and 3 per cent for girls, but by 1967 these had doubled,
to 23 per cent and 8 per cent respectively.

What emerges from this chapter? Has the effort of forecasting
been worth it? There is one school of thought which is sceptical
of forecasts and rejoices when they are wrong: this, they argue,
just goes to show the importance of introducing the maxi-
mum of flexibility and of private initiative into the system, for
planning based on forecasts will be planning based on wrong
forecasts.

Against this is the argument that an unplanned system would
have been far less capable of handling the bulge. One can of
course argue that the private demand for places, and hence the
bulge, is irrelevant. But most people would agree that in the short
run there is a strong social case for preserving equal opportunities for children, irrespective of the size of the age group to
which chance has allotted them – to disappoint expectations is
costly. If this is granted, there is no alternative to forecasting.

The battle of the bulge was won in large measure because of the comparative accuracy of the forecasts. But these would have been useless without the response of the institutions of higher education.

Chapter Four
University Expansion

The Robbins Committee's five-year plan for crash action to meet the crisis of the bulge, involved a radical revision of the universities' expansion plans. Before the *Robbins Report,* the number of places planned for 1967–8 was 172,000: the *Report* asked for 197,000. As soon as the *Report* was out, Sir John Wolfenden, the new Chairman of the University Grants Committee, wrote to the universities asking them what they could do to help achieve the new target, and how much it would cost them. The required increase in places amounted to 40 per cent over four years. Yet in their replies the universities said they could provide some 20,000 places more than the 197,000 needed – a magnificent response which considerably surprised those who hold a general belief that universities are impervious to social need. The response was undoubtedly influenced by the euphoric atmosphere induced by the publication of the *Robbins Report,* and also by the opportunities for building up new lines of activity offered by such an expansion. It did, however, dispel, one hopes for ever, the picture of universities as exclusive clubs which cannot bear to expand their membership. When we are thinking of the fact that other sectors have expanded faster than the universities, we should not forget that this is by the wish of the government and not of the universities.

The government and the U.G.C. agreed that 197,000 was the limit. At the time this was a reasonable decision though it disappointed many of those universities whose offers were partly rejected. It may be that, in future exercises of this kind, it will prove better if the U.G.C. gives a more definite advance indication of the kind of expansion which might be suitable for each university. In any case, the quinquennial grants for the years up to 1966–7 were duly adjusted to provide for the Robbins targets for student numbers. These targets have been achieved almost to the letter as Figure 2 showed.

Some people imagine that the main expansion has been in the new universities or in the colleges of advanced technology, which were formally promoted into the university club in 1965. But though the rates of growth here have been very high, the bulk of the extra places have in fact been provided in the older civic universities, that is, those already existing before the first 'new' university, at Sussex, opened its doors in 1961. Since 1962–3, student numbers have grown by 69,000: of these, 12,000 were in new universities, 10,000 in former colleges of advanced technology, 2,500 at Oxford and Cambridge, 6,000 at London, 3,500 in Wales, 10,000 in Scotland, and all the other 25,000 in the older English civic universities. These figures are shown graphically in Figure 1 facing the title page. The colleges of advanced technology have doubled their full-time numbers from 10,000 to 20,000, but it is interesting to see that advanced work in the technical colleges remaining in the further education sector grew even faster than this.

What has all this expansion done to the opportunities for university entry? We have already looked at this rather broadly, but a more searching look is needed. There is, let us face it, a problem. In 1965 the colleges of advanced technology became universities by a stroke of the pen. This did not in itself add to the provision of real university-level educational facilities, and in order to obtain a consistent time series we have, as already explained, included the C.A.T.s in with the universities in all years, before and after 1965. But of course, in so far as the C.A.T.s have bit by bit transformed the quality of their work, this procedure has the effect of understating the true increase in university-level opportunities.

But sticking to this procedure, we find that since 1962 the proportion of leavers with two or more A levels who go to university has been more or less constant around 58 per cent, having fallen from 65 per cent in 1961. Before the bulge hit the universities, the girls' schools were worried that their pupils might get squeezed out. In fact girls seem to have done no worse in the crisis than boys. Although the number of girls with A levels has grown faster than boys, the number of them entering university has also grown faster. But it is still true that a much smaller proportion of girls with A level go to university than the corresponding proportion for boys – 44 per cent compared with 67 per cent (see Table 7).

Table 7

Home Initial Entrants to Universities (Including Former C.A.T.s) as Percentage of Those with Two or More A Levels, Entrants from England and Wales

	Men	Women	Men and women
1961	74	49	65
1962	68	44	59
1963	67	45	59
1964	67	44	59
1965	66	44	57
1966	65	44	57
1967	67	44	58

As compared with Robbins, the number of entrants (except in 1967) has been almost exactly as recommended, but of course the numbers of school leavers with A level has been higher, by as much as 26 per cent in 1967. Thus the proportion of 'qualified school leavers' entering university has fallen by about 10 per cent of itself since 1961. There is still a good case for getting back to the 1961 proportion.

The recent U.G.C. quinquennial settlement for the years 1967–8 to 1971–2 does not achieve this. It provides for an increase of about 20,000 places over the Robbins targets for 1971–2: 220,000 to 225,000 places being the new official target.[1] But by that year we can expect (using the Department's latest projection) an output of people with two or more A levels some 21 per cent higher than Robbins. This implies that the entry rate in 1971 will still be only some 90 per cent of its 1961 value.

Opportunities ought really of course to be related to the numbers of suitably qualified people who *wish* to go rather than simply to the numbers having the relevant qualifications. Unfortunately the evidence on the growth of university applicants over time is shaky, because the coverage of the scheme run by the

Universities Central Council on Admissions has been steadily widened, so that comparisons over time are difficult. But we estimate that the proportion of school leavers with two or more A levels who applied to university for the first time was 77 per cent plus or minus 1 per cent, in each of the years 1963, 1964 and 1965.[2] And of those with these qualifications who applied, about 62 per cent were accepted in every year – as Table 8 shows.[3] Thus we were in fact right when we inferred from the constant entry rate to universities (in Table 1) that the degree of competition among those who applied has been more or less constant.

Table 8

The Acceptance Rate: Percentage of Candidates through U.C.C.A. with Two or More A Levels who are Accepted, Great Britain

	1963	1964	1965	1966
Humanities	58	59	57	58
Social studies	51	52	52	48
All arts	56	57	54	53
Pure science	66	71	77	80
Applied science	73	72	78	74
Medicine	51	50	50	54
All science	67	67	73	74
Other	57	63	60	57
Total	62	62	63	62

However, if we look at the position in different faculties the scene changes. Acceptance rates have fallen in arts faculties (taking arts to include both humanities and social studies), while they have risen in science faculties. It is in social sciences that the real pinch has come, for although, as we shall see, expansion there has been faster than in any other faculty the rush of applicants has grown even faster. By contrast, acceptance rates have risen sharply in pure science. Why is this?

Chapter Five
The Swing from Science

In the 1950s the study of natural sciences grew faster, in schools and universities, than any other branch of learning. This role has now been taken by the social sciences. At A level, for example, output grew much faster in science than arts until 1959, but then the arts backlash began. This was first noticed in the *Robbins Report,* but, perhaps unfortunately, no forecast was made of its future course. Since then the swing back has continued, with economics in the lead.[1]

Suppose we take those with two or more A levels and divide them between arts and science, allocating fifty-fifty those with a mixture of arts and science subjects – such students still unhappily amount to only 14 per cent of the total. We get the picture shown in Table 9. While the numbers specializing in arts

Table 9

School Leavers with Two or More A Levels: by Subject Group, England and Wales (Thousands)

	Boys		Girls		Boys and girls	
	Arts	Science	Arts	Science	Arts	Science
1961	10·8	16·8	11·0	4·7	21·8	21·5
1967	23·6	25·3	23·0	7·4	46·7	32·6
Percentage growth	119	51	109	57	114	52

have grown by 114 per cent, those in science have grown by only 52 per cent. Or, looked at another way, the proportion specializing in arts has risen from 50 per cent to 59 per cent, as we show in Figure 9.

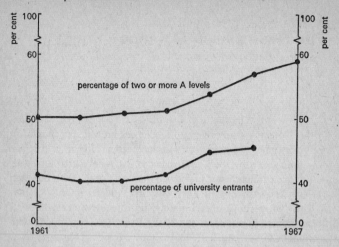

Figure 9. Percentage of those with two or more A levels specializing in arts, and percentage of university entrants studying arts, entrants from England and Wales

How have the universities reacted? From the middle of the 1950s until 1967 official U.G.C. policy, justified by arguments of manpower need, was that two-thirds of all additional university places should be in science and technology – which meant that these subjects should grow a great deal faster than others. But in fact the universities, faced by a completely unexpected swing of applicants from science to arts, have very largely adapted to it, though not completely.

As Figure 9 shows, the trend in university entry has largely followed the trend in the schools, the proportion reading arts having risen, but relatively not quite as much as the proportion of A level students qualified in arts. As a result the chances of university entry have worsened slightly for school leavers qualified in arts relative to those qualified in science. This is brought out in Table 10. The pattern of entry rates thus corresponds broadly to the pattern of acceptance rates that we saw in the last chapter. We should emphasize that this is not a statistical artefact due to the translation of the C.A.T.s into universities. For entrants to C.A.T.s are included in all years; and

Table 10

Home Entrants to Universities (Including Former C.A.T.s):
by Subject Group, Entrants from England and Wales

	Numbers (thousands)		As percentage of school leavers with two or more A levels	
	Arts	Science	Arts	Science
1961	11·7	16·6	54	77
1962	12·2	18·0	48	71
1963	12·8	18·8	47	72
1964	14·8	20·9	48	71
1965	18·9	23·1	48	68
1966	19·7	23·5	46	72

if we exclude them in all years the picture is the same: opportunities in science subjects did not diminish while those in arts did slightly. And if we could also take into account the improvement in C.A.T. courses, the picture of the changing opportunities in science would be even rosier.

In terms of extra places from 1961–2 to 1966–7, the universities (excluding former C.A.T.s) have provided only 37 per cent of them in science and technology, compared with the two-thirds planned. If C.A.T.s are included in both years the figure is still only 43 per cent. As a result the proportion of places in arts subjects has risen from 40 to 44 per cent, instead of falling to 37 per cent as recommended by Robbins (see Table 11).[2]

How are we to interpret this outcome? It is undoubtedly a failure of planning. In the first place, capital expenditure on science relative to arts has been higher than it would have been had the pattern of student intake been correctly foreseen. Moreover, one objective of educational planning must surely be to minimize private disappointment by harmonizing the pattern of education at one level with that at another.[3]

The practical difficulty here is that paradoxically the universities, which are often thought to be outside social control, are in fact much more centrally planned than the schools. There is

Table 11

Full-time Students in Universities (Including Former C.A.T.s): by Faculty, Great Britain

	Arts	Pure science	Applied science	Medicine	Agriculture	Total
Number (thousands)						
Actual						
1961–2	49·3	31·4	24·1	16·6	2·1	123·4
1966–7	81·3	44·4	37·0	18·9	2·5	184·2
Robbins						
1966–7	*68·9*	*52·7*	*43·8*	*19·0*	*2·5*	*186·9*
Percentage of students						
Actual						
1961–2	40·0	25·4	19·5	13·4	1·7	100·0
1966–7	44·1	24·1	20·1	10·3	1·4	100·0
Robbins						
1966–7	*36·9*	*28·2*	*23·4*	*10·2*	*1·3*	*100·0*

no advance planning of the size of sixth forms, still less of their subject balance. One reason for this is, of course, that the sixth forms constitute a small part of the school population and substantial changes in them can be fairly easily absorbed. The main instrument of British educational planning is the control of capital expenditure, but most sixth forms have no specific buildings, and therefore those who sanction capital expenditure are not required to form a view about sixth forms; nor, if they had a view, would they have any ready means of implementing it.

There seem two ways out of this situation:

(a) To take an active manpower-oriented policy in the schools, or

(b) To stop taking one in the universities.

The U.G.C. have now overtly opted for (b). For the first time they issued (in November 1967), a 'Memorandum of general guidance' explaining the general ideas lying behind the allocations of the final quinquennial settlement, announced the same month.[4] This is what the statement said about the subject balance: 'The Committee have taken the view that in the light of present A level trends the major increase must be in the number of arts-based, rather than science-based, students.' Among other surprising results, this has had the effect of sharply restricting the prospective growth of the former Colleges of Advanced Technology, which, had they not become universities, would now be a major focus of expansion.

A different approach informs the Report of the Dainton Committee. They believe that the swing is highly undesirable, and that it must be halted by an active policy in the schools. This argument is based largely on the evidence of the *Triennial Manpower Survey of Engineers, Technologists, Scientists and Technical Supporting Staff*.[5] This survey collects evidence on employers' opinions about short-term demands. Such evidence is difficult to interpret, and it is necessary at least to consider the alternative argument that an accelerated production of scientists and engineers would require an over-investment in those sectors of education.

In short, it is desirable to look at the economics of the swing. This involves knowing the salary differentials between graduates in different subjects, and it is unfortunate that we do not yet have usable statistics on these.[6] But common observation suggests that, if scientists and engineers do command any premium, it is not large.[7] And scientists and engineers cost a lot more to produce than arts graduates. So if each group of graduates were being paid the value of their (marginal) product, it would seem to follow that society's rate of return is just as high in producing arts as science graduates.

But are graduates being paid their economic value? The average salaries of arts graduates are strongly influenced by the salaries of the high proportion of them who are in the teaching profession, this being much less true for science teachers. Now the teaching profession is remarkable in its insistence that teachers shall be paid similarly in all subjects,[8] regardless of the state of supply and demand in different fields. As a result, a shortage of graduate science teachers may lead to a pay rise for teachers of modern languages – the purpose of the rise being to make science teachers' pay competitive with the pay of scientists in industry. This must be an extremely important mechanism for equating the prospects of arts and science graduates. It also brings home the dangers of inferring the true value of a person's work from his actual rate of pay. For this reason the broad conclusions of the Dainton Committee seem to us right and important. The country may not be notably short of scientific specialists, but it is very likely that good returns could be got from increasing the level of general scientific understanding among educated people. Mathematics has a key role in this, and the greatest manpower bottleneck in the country now is probably the shortage of mathematics teachers to implement the Dainton recommendation of mathematics for all in the sixth forms.

Apart from proposing that the broad balance between faculties should be tilted in favour of science and, especially, technology, the Robbins Committee recommended one other major new development that was intended to boost the status of technology not only relative to arts but also relative to pure science. The argument was that, even if Britain were producing enough average-level technologists, we were not producing enough really good ones. As the figures on A level grades show, brilliant students tended, and still tend, to go for pure rather than applied science,[9] and this may help to account for the failure of basic research to get translated into commercial projects as effectively here as in other countries.

To counter this, Robbins proposed the creation of five so-called S.I.S.T.E.R.s – Special Institutions for Scientific and Technological Education and Research, sometimes unofficially referred to as super-C.A.T.s or Tigers. Apart from the name, the proposal was very attractive. Four of the institutions were to be based on existing colleges in London (Imperial College), Manchester and Glasgow and on one of the C.A.T.s. But the fifth, which might have had the largest impact on public opinion, was to be new.

The S.I.S.T.E.R.s proposal has never got off the ground – the pressures against such overt discrimination were too great. But more seriously, no new high-level institution, no British M.I.T., has appeared to capture the public imagination. This is partly because of one of the first decisions made by the Labour Government in 1964, which was perfectly justifiable at the time.

Robbins had proposed the founding of six new universities. This was based on the estimated need for places in 1980–81, which, when compared with a U.G.C. estimate of the potential of existing institutions by that time, left an excess of 30,000 places. These the Committee said should be provided in six further universities, of which the new S.I.S.T.E.R. should be one. In the event the 'overbidding' by the universities in their immediate response to the *Robbins Report* led the government to think that the U.G.C. might have also underestimated the potential capacity of existing universities in 1980–81. For this reason, and because of its 'binary' philosophy (more, on which, below), the government rejected the idea of the six further universities, and with it the idea of the new S.I.S.T.E.R. The higher trend in A level output might, however, make them think again about this one specific proposal, which might yet have a major contribution to make to the health of the economy.

But whatever the desirable pattern of higher education, the problem remains of ensuring that the sixth forms develop in step with it. One approach might, by the use of vocational guidance or even subject quotas, guide the right number of sixth formers into each of the specialist boxes. This seems to us quite wrong. For it is the unhealthy extent of sixth form specialization in Britain which is the source of many of these problems. The Dainton Committee wanted reduced specialization, and the universal study of mathematics in sixth forms, largely, as a way of extending the pool from which science and technology undergraduates can be drawn. But the case exists quite independently of the subject balance in higher education. As the Robbins Committee said:

We do not believe, for example, that it is in the public interest that a student of natural science or technology is frequently not competent in even one foreign language, a student of economics is often without the desirable complement of mathematics and a student of history or literature may be unaware of the significance of science and the scientific method.[10]

In the same vein the *Swann Report* has recently recommended that at the university level

to meet current and future needs of employment, and to give students of science, engineering and technology some understanding of the society in which they will work, universities should consider making the first degree course in science, engineering and technology, broad in character, through multi-disciplinary approaches to these subjects and by introducing relevant study in other fields such as economics, sociology, law, etc.[11]

Why do these changes take so long to come about?[12] Partly by inertia, but partly because of genuine disagreement. For example *The Times* disagreed flatly with parts of the *Swann Report*: 'We do need general scientists with a range of scientfic disciplines' it commented, 'but we do not need scientists with a smattering of social science disciplines.'[13] At this rate it may take some time before specialization is very much reduced.

Chapter Six
Postgraduate Studies and
Overseas Students

The corollary of later specialization is longer education. The Robbins Committee recognized this,[1] and Chapter 8 of their *Report* includes a panegyric on the merits of postgraduate study. The most powerful reason for developing postgraduate work is of course the growth of knowledge. Robbins argued that this does not mean that undergraduate courses need be lengthened: instead people should cease pretending that undergraduates can reach the frontiers of knowledge. Students who want to become professionals in the fullest sense will have to take postgraduate courses as they do in the United States. These should be real courses, with an examined syllabus and a programme of teaching; there is much less need for an expansion in the numbers doing research degrees.

Developments since the *Robbins Report* have closely followed this pattern. First, a growing proportion of graduates have stayed on to do postgraduate study, and in fact the proportion has grown even faster than Robbins suggested. Not counting those going on to the Postgraduate Certificate in Education, or Dip. Ed., as it is colloquially called, the proportion going on in 1961 was 20 per cent; Robbins suggested it should rise to 30 per cent by 1980 – an average annual rise of $\frac{1}{2}$ per cent, equal to 2·5 per cent of the 1961 level. Unfortunately the U.G.C. statistics do not provide a directly comparable figure of what has happened, but we can arrive at one by a roundabout route. Taking all home postgraduates and expressing them as a proportion of students graduating in the previous summer, we get the results shown in Table 12. Between 1961–2 and 1966–7 the proportion rose from 45 to 60 per cent – an average annual increment of 3·0 percentage points, equal to 6·6 per cent of the 1961 level. Thus the actual rate of growth of staying on, as measured by our roundabout method, has been 6·6 per cent a year compared with the 2·5 per cent recommended. If the average period for which people stay on has fallen, as more take their degrees by short periods of 'course-work' rather than long periods of thesis writing, then the proportion staying on must have risen even more than 6·6 per cent a year.

Table 12
Home Full-time Postgraduates, Excluding Teacher Training, as Percentage of Students Graduating in the Previous Year, Great Britain[2]

	1961–2	1962–3	1963–4	1964–5	1965–6	1966–7
Percentage	44·7	46·2	49·6	53·8	55·9	59·5

By contrast, the average undergraduate length of course has remained practically constant. The number of home undergraduates in each year since 1961–2 has been slightly greater than the sum of the undergraduate entrants in the three most recent years. If the excess is expressed as a proportion of entrants three years earlier, it always lies between 8 and 11 per cent – another of the remarkable stabilities in educational statistics.[3] Since rates of wastage and of repeating years of the course have been very stable over a long period,[4] this means that there has been no change in the standard length of the undergraduate course.

Granted the increasing proportions going on to postgraduate study we should expect to find postgraduates forming an ever growing proportion of the student body. This is in fact what has happened: leaving out former C.A.T.s, postgraduates increased as a proportion of all home students from 13·2 per cent in 1962–3 to 14·4 per cent in 1966–7. We cannot do this sum separately by faculty unless we include overseas students who formed, in 1966–7, 29 per cent of all the postgraduate students in the country. Including them, we find the proportion of postgraduates has risen in every faculty – most strikingly of all in applied science (see Table 13). In applied and pure science the proportion is now over 20 per cent, compared with only 14 per cent in social sciences. In medicine only 8 per cent are postgraduates: though

Table 13

Postgraduates as Percentage of all Full-time University Students, Great Britain

	Humanities	Social studies	All arts	Pure science	Applied science	Medicine	Agriculture	Total
1962–3	10·9	15·7	12·3	19·9	17·8	8·5	15·7	14·8
1963–4	11·3	16·1	12·8	20·1	19·2	8·6	14·3	15·3
1964–5	12·6	16·5	13·7	21·3	19·9	8·4	16·8	16·1
1965–6	13·2*	12·8*	13·0	20·8	19·9	8·5	16·7	15·7
1966–7	14·6*	13·8*	14·2	20·9	20·6	8·2	18·6	16·3

*The dividing line between humanities and social studies was redrawn in 1965–6.[6]

the undergraduate course is unusually long, postgraduate provision is poor, as the Royal Commission on Medical Education has recently pointed out.[5]

What are all the postgraduates doing? Has the Robbins recommendation for more course work, compared with research, been followed? On the whole, yes. If we leave out Education,[7] 30 per cent of all postgraduates in 1966-7 were doing courses, compared with only 24 per cent in 1961-2. The pattern of postgraduate work varies tremendously between faculties: the proportion on courses is over half in social studies (55 per cent) and medicine (51 per cent), and under a third in applied science (32 per cent) and humanities (28 per cent). In pure science all but 12 per cent are doing research. Between 1961-2 and 1966-7 the proportion doing courses has risen in every faculty by between 4 and 9 percentage points except in medicine where it has fallen.

Unfortunately we cannot distinguish postgraduates who have gone on more or less directly after graduation from those who have done a job, and then returned to master some new specialization, or to catch up with new developments in their subject. Sir Eric Ashby once suggested that all degrees should be cancelled after a number of years on grounds of their technological obsolescence. One can imagine one or two people objecting to this; but it seems likely that among the biggest of all impending changes in university life, will be the growing number of older students coming back to recharge their batteries.

Even so, is the recent rate of growth of postgraduate study an unmixed blessing? The U.G.C. think not, and in making their quinquennial allocations 'have consciously taken the view that undergraduate numbers are a genuine priority.'[8] In this they have been strongly influenced by a growing school of thought among scientists typified in the *Swann Committee's Report*. According to this, the effect of postgraduate study, and especially of the Ph.D. as it exists at present, is to direct too many of our best scientists and engineers to careers in research rather than in industrial production or school teaching, where the greatest shortages exist. The evidence for this view is strong and we would not argue with it. But it seems quite doubtful whether the same line of argument applies in, for example, the social sciences. Postgraduate study is far less common in these subjects – as we have seen, only 14 per cent of students are postgraduates compared with over 20 per cent in science and technology, and the difference is even greater if overseas students are excluded. The demand for professionally competent social scientists is extremely high and it is increasingly difficult to be professionally competent without some postgraduate training. It will therefore be a pity if the limits on postgraduate expansion are applied indiscriminately.

Most of this study has so far been concerned with students from this country. We have seen how the Robbins Committee worked out the number of places for home undergraduate entrants, and the number of these going on to postgraduate study. But overseas students raise quite different questions. Demographic fluctuations abroad, and certainly in the underdeveloped world, do not coincide with those in this country. And even in the long term it is not obvious that the growth in overseas students ought to be related to the growth in the number of home students. However, it happens that up to 1961–2 the number of overseas students had in fact grown at almost the same rate as the number of home students. The reasons for this are complex but the main explanation must lie in the educational explosion in the underdeveloped countries of Asia, Africa and Latin America, which in 1962–3 supplied 70 per cent of overseas students in British universities. Faced with the rising tide of applicants from these countries, British universities seem to have judged that the least they could do would be to share a stable proportion of their extra facilities with students from the poorer half of the world. The government seems to have concurred in this form of foreign aid, in the sense that it did nothing to recover from overseas students the subsidy they received by paying fees far below cost: by 1962–3 the total subsidy in all institutions of higher education amounted to nearly £10 million.

Faced with the problem of estimating future provision for overseas students, the Robbins Committee decided that the best procedure would be to assume constant (1961–2) proportions in the future as in the past. They also predicted that in universities a growing proportion of overseas students would be postgraduates.

The latter prediction has been fulfilled, but the former prescription has not. The position is shown in Table 14. Since 1961–2 the

Table 14

Overseas Full-time Students in Universities (Excluding Former C.A.T.s), Great Britain[9]

	Overseas students (number)			Overseas as a percentage of all full-time students		
	Undergraduates	Postgraduates	Total	Undergraduates	Postgraduates	Total
1957–8	5,950	4,210	10,160	7·3	29·9	10·6
1958–9	5,920	4,280	10,200	6·9	28·8	10·2
1959–60	5,940	4,710	10,650	6·8	28·3	10·2
1960–1	6,380	5,230	11,610	7·1	29·3	10·8
1961–2	6,920	6,110	13,020	7·4	31·5	11·5
1962–3	6,480	6,890	13,380	6·6	33·2	11·2
1963–4	6,520	7,270	13,790	6·3	32·2	10·9
1964–5	6,620	7,870	14,480	5·8	30·8	10·4
1965–6	6,650	7,830	14,480	5·3	28·8	9·5
1966–7	6,820	8,720	15,550	5·1	28·7	9·4

proportion of overseas students has fallen from 11·5 per cent to 9·4 per cent. The number of overseas undergraduates has not grown at all, and overseas postgraduates, though growing in number, have fallen from 32 to 29 per cent of the total. Overseas students now form very roughly a third of all postgraduates in each faculty except medicine, where they form two-thirds, and pure science where they are only a fifth. The fall in the postgraduate proportion has occurred in all faculties except medicine, but mainly in social science and humanities.

These changes partly result from the advice which the Chairman of the U.G.C. gave to Vice-Chancellors in the letter he wrote just after the publication of the *Robbins Report*. In it he said:

In the emergency period up to 1967–8 the Committee feel that the universities will not dissent from the view that priority should be given to the increase in the home demand, on which the Robbins figures now adopted were calculated; and that a corresponding proportionate increase in the intake of overseas students could not be expected.

More recently there has been another step that is likely to retard further the expansion of overseas numbers. In December 1966, Mr Anthony Crosland announced that fees for overseas students were to be raised from the general average of £70 for home and overseas students to £250 – or, to be more precise that the U.G.C. grant to each university would be computed on the assumption that it would raise fees in this way. Most, but not all, universities have done this. There was, however, a spontaneous protest against the change, especially from British students, who stood to gain nothing from protesting. As a result of this, and of the remonstrations of the Vice-Chancellors, a hardship fund has been set up to help overseas students who have difficulty paying the fees. The money in the fund is, however, a good deal less than the extra money raised in fees, and the change is therefore a cut in foreign aid. Against this it is true that many overseas students, even from poor countries, are from rich families, and aid to them accentuates rather than reduces income inequality. Even so, the measure as it now stands is bound to have reduced the attractions of Britain to students from poor countries, which seems a pity both from a moral point of view, and possibly from the point of view of diplomatic relations and export markets.

Many of Britain's overseas students are not of course in universities. In 1966–7 there were, as well as the 16,760 in universities, 500 in colleges of education and 7,060 on 'advanced' full-time courses in further education. The numbers in colleges of education have always been small, and they have in fact fallen from 675 in 1962–3 to their present 500: the policy has been to take the trainers of teachers rather than the teachers themselves, so as to secure the largest possible effect for each person trained. In further education the numbers have risen considerably, from 4,540 in 1962–3 to 7,060, but the proportion has fallen from 16·2 to 13·0 per cent. Considering the fantastic expansion of home students, this fall is hardly surprising; but this does not mean that it need continue.

Chapter Seven
The Binary System

Books on higher education used to begin and end with the universities. We have begun with them but we shall not end there. For though the oldest, the universities are the slowest growing part of higher education. In 1962–3 they provided 60 per cent of the places and the Robbins Committee recommended maintaining this: but their actual share had fallen to 53 per cent by 1967–8. For when the number of well-qualified school leavers rose above the Robbins prediction, the government stuck to the Robbins number of places and the increased supply of students went into the non-university sector. This was no accidental outcome. Behind it lay a fundamental divergence between the government's and the Robbins Committee's view of the role of the universities in the system of higher education.

This book is not about the qualitative and administrative recommendations of the *Robbins Report* nor about the extent to which they have been implemented. But the issue of the 'binary system' has major quantitative as well as administrative implications, and must be looked at.

As we said earlier, the quantitative aspects of the *Robbins Report* were accepted by the government at the outset, and have left a major impact on national history. A good number of the administrative recommendations were also accepted – for example the turning of the Colleges of Advanced Technology into universities, the establishment of the Council for National Academic Awards, and the introduction of a B.Ed. in colleges of education.

But two of the most important administrative proposals were ultimately rejected. First, where Robbins had opted for two Ministries (one for universities and science, and another for the rest of education) the Conservative Government decided, after some months of deliberation and political infighting, to have a unified Department of Education and Science.[1] This decision must have affected the quantitative development of higher education, but it is impossible to tell whether it promoted or discouraged it.

The second major administrative decision going against the Robbins recommendations was left to the Labour Government and its Secretary of State, Mr Michael Stewart. The Robbins Committee had recommended that the colleges of education should become parts of universities, being federated into University Schools of Education. Each school would be financed through its university and would be academically responsible to the Senate. After over a year's discussion the colleges and the universities (or nearly all of them) came out in favour of the marriage, but the government raised an impediment and, on the advice of the University Grants Committee, decided that 'for the present the colleges should continue to be administered by the existing maintaining bodies.'[2] There were a number of weighty practical, as well as the more philosophical, arguments in favour of this decision – in particular the argument that, in a period of acute shortage of primary (and especially of infant) school teachers, it could be disastrous to remove the colleges from relatively direct ministerial control.

But the period of acute shortage will pass, and it was therefore encouraging to note the phrase 'for the present' in the official announcement. However, it was only months after this announcement that Mr Stewart's successor, Mr Crosland enunciated, in a speech at the Woolwich Polytechnic, a new principle to underline future government policy, which implied that the divorce between the universities and the rest of higher education was to be regarded as permanent.[3]

This was the 'binary' principle, which said in essence that there should be two systems of higher education at degree level, one in the autonomous sector (the universities) and one in the publicly-controlled sector (the technical colleges, and, for B.Ed. courses, the colleges of education); and the second should be developed more rapidly than the first.

The issues involved here were and remain extremely complex, powerful arguments existing for and against the policy. This is not the place to do more than record them in summary form.

The arguments in favour of the policy include the following:

1. Universities are unwilling to develop applied studies at a high level on a large enough scale, and are correspondingly remote from industry and commerce.

2. Universities provide little part-time education and it is vital for part-time students that they can be taught in institutions which also provide high quality full-time education. There is also a case for comprehensive institutions doing lower as well as higher level work.

3. Bright young people from working class homes are either put off by universities or have qualifications (such as Ordinary National Certificate) which universities will not accept as satisfying entry requirements.

4. Universities are not sufficiently accessible to government control for these evils to be remedied.

5. The unit cost of producing a comparably educated student is less in a technical college than a university.

Some of the arguments against the policy are:

1. Only the universities can give real status to applied studies.

2. Students will continue to put universities as their first choice; binary policy by restricting university places will intensify the unhealthy competition for university entry.

3. A binary policy involves dispersion of resources on too many institutions and fails to reap the economies of placing large numbers of students in contact with the best academic minds, most of whom may want to work in universities.

4. There is no evidence that it is cheaper on average to produce graduates in technical colleges than in universities, even if we include the cost of university research in the cost of producing graduates; in terms of marginal costs it may be less sensible to expand relatively small colleges with staffs appointed for lesser responsibilities, than to create new universities.

Without elaborating on the debate, we cannot help expressing our view that the binary philosophy is wrong and that, insofar as it is implemented, it will involve a greater waste of national resources than a policy in which the universities were given a larger role.[4]

It is still early days and the policy has so far been implemented only in part. Its main specific expression is the plan to create thirty polytechnics of ultimately around 2,000 full-time students each.[5] These will be based on existing technical colleges and their staffs, though it seems that a considerable number of them will in fact involve a physical change of site. However, on top of this, further education and teacher training have already been expanded a great deal faster than the universities. It is time to look at the remarkable achievements in these sectors.

Chapter Eight
The Colleges of Education

If there were a prize to be awarded for expansion, it would have to go to the colleges of education. Unlike the further education colleges, they cannot expand their numbers of advanced students by using up space previously occupied by non-advanced students. Nor have many new colleges been founded. So more students has meant larger colleges. And student numbers have doubled in five years.

Since the peaceful, and even stagnant, days of the 1950s the colleges in England and Wales have been subjected to three main waves of expansion. The first came when it was decided to lengthen the basic course from two to three years for students entering in 1960. This had the effect of expanding the colleges by a third in the autumn of 1962.

One reason why the course was lengthened was that, when the decision was taken in the late 1950s, the teacher supply situation was thought to be well in hand. Nothing could have been further from the truth. From the middle fifties onwards, the falling age of marriage increased the numbers of children being born, and at the same time aggravated the wastage rate of women teachers. The resulting crisis in the primary schools gave rise to the so-called '80,000 place programme', announced while the Robbins Committee was sitting, which aimed at about 80,000 places in England and Wales by 1970–71.[1] It was soon clear that even this might well not be enough. The Robbins Committee considered whether to recommend raising the target but were told by the Ministry of Education that, given the constraints of buildings, staff and the adaptive capacity of the colleges, it would be impossible to go above this plan in any year before 1969. However, from that year onwards the Committee recommended a further steep increase to 111,000 places by 1973–4.

In the event the Robbins recommendations, and by the same

token the 80,000 place programme, have been greatly exceeded –
by about 26 per cent by 1967–8. This has stemmed from the third
expansionary push to which the colleges have been subjected.
In 1965 the National Advisory Council on the Training and
Supply of Teachers produced their ninth report which showed,
even more clearly than the forecasts in Robbins, the gravity of
the teacher situation.[2] The Department of Education had long
been interested in the possibilities of increasing the productivity
of the colleges. After receiving the Council's calculations, Mr
Crosland asked the colleges to prepare plans for using their
buildings (already existing and planned) to house 20 per cent
more students than originally envisaged.[3] Their recurrent
finance was to be adjusted so that the staff/student ratio was
maintained. As a result the number of places has risen to 95,000
in 1967–8 compared with 75,000 in the 80,000-place plan. In
Scotland too the Robbins plan has been substantially overshot.
These contrasts are shown in Table 15.

Table 15

Students in Colleges of Education, Great Britain

| | England and Wales | | Scotland | |
	Actual	Robbins	Actual	Robbins
1961–2	36,500	.	5,700	.
1962–3	48,400	.	6,300	.
1963–4	54,800	52,800	7,100	6,400
1964–5	62,800	58,900	7,900	7,000
1965–6	73,300	66,000	8,900	7,900
1966–7	85,500	71,100	9,700	8,500
1967–8	94,800	75,200	10,800	9,000

One might think that such an astonishing expansion would
inevitably be accompanied by a declining quality of entrants.
But, as Table 16 shows, there has been no significant fall in the
proportion of entrants having A levels. The proportion of women
with less than five O levels has grown slightly, but these are
mainly older married women.

Table 16

The Percentage of Entrants to Colleges of Education Having Different Qualifications, England and Wales

	Two or more A levels	One A level	Five or more O levels but no A levels	Others	Total
Men					
1961	39	23	28	9	100
1967	37	25	27	11	100
Women					
1961	36	23	32	8	100
1967	35	24	28	13	100
Men and women					
1961	37	23	31	8	100
1967	36	24	28	12	100

How in fact have the qualifications of entrants been maintained? The answer is simple. It is mainly because of the unexpected upsurge at A level. On top of this there has been some increase in the proportions of A level leavers going to the colleges. This can be seen from Table 17, in which we have analysed entrants to each sector of higher education according to their qualifications, and then expressed the number of entrants as a proportion of the output of school leavers with those qualifications in the same year. For the time being we are only concerned with the proportions in the column marked colleges of education. Among A level leavers, and even more among those with O levels only, there has been some increase in the proportions going to colleges of education. For A levels the increase is confined to women, but for O levels it applies to men as well.

Why have these proportions increased? Is it because higher proportions apply or because more of the applicants are admitted? We do not know in what proportions people are applying. If we assume that most A level applicants are accepted, then

Table 17

Home Initial Entrants to Full-time Higher Education as Percentage of those with G.C.E. Qualifications, Entrants from England and Wales[4]

	Universities (excluding former C.A.T.s)	Former C.A.T.s	Colleges of education	Further education	No full-time higher education	All with G.C.E.
Two or more A levels						
1961	59	4	14	5	18	100
1962	53	5	13	5	24	100
1963	52	6	16	6	20	100
1964	52	7	15	6	21	100
1965	50	7	16	6	21	100
1966	50	7	16	7	20	100
1967	51	8	16	8	18	100
One A level						
1961	—	3	28	12	57	100
1962	—	2	27	13	57	100
1963	—	2	30	14	54	100
1964	—	1	31	15	54	100
1965	—	—	32	14	54	100
1966	—	—	32	15	53	100
1967	—	—	32	18	50	100

Five or more O levels
but no A levels

1961	—	—	1	12	2	85	100
1962	—	—	11	2	87	100
1963	—	—	12	2	85	100
1964	—	—	15	3	83	100
1965	—	—	15	3	82	100
1966	—	—	17	3	80	100
1967	—	—	19	4	76	100

presumably more have been applying – as a result of increased competition for university entry. But it also seems that at the margin there may have been slackening of standards of selection. Applicants are classified as 'qualified' or 'unqualified' by a panel of scrutineers at the colleges' Clearing House. Of those deemed qualified a rather smaller proportion were refused a place after 1964 than before – but, as Table 18 shows, the difference is relatively small.

Table 18

Percentage of Qualified Applicants (Other than Those Withdrawing their Applications) not Admitted to Colleges of Education, Applicants from England and Wales

	1961	1962	1963	1964	1965	1966	1967
Men	17	19	19	17	14	10	14
Women	10	17	9	6	8	6	5
Men and women	12	17	12	9	10	7	8

Since the three-year course was begun, the effective length of course in the colleges in England and Wales has been very stable: student numbers in each year since 1962–3 have equalled the last two years' intake, plus between 85 and 95 per cent of the intake the year before that. In Scotland there has been more fluctuation – the law of large numbers applies less strictly, but there is no trend up or down. Thus the number of entrants and the number of places have expanded *pari passu*.

Chapter Nine
Further Education

Further education is the *omnium gatherum* part of post-school education, catering for more than a million students, some full-time but mostly part-time, at levels varying from postgraduate courses to craftsman training. We are only concerned with the academic tip of this iceberg, with people taking so-called 'advanced' courses, which are above the level of G.C.E. A level or of the Ordinary National Certificate. And we only look at full-time students, roughly a third of all the advanced students. Even so, the students we are interested in are studying in a wide variety of types of college – polytechnics, technical colleges, art colleges and so on. And in all these colleges they share the same buildings and teachers as part-timers, and in most cases as students on non-advanced courses.

Since Robbins, the increase in advanced full-time students in the colleges has been very striking and, as in the colleges of education, has far exceeded the Robbins targets – but through a quite different mechanism. Further education has always since the War acted as the safety valve for higher education, mopping up the demand not satisfied in the other sectors. There are many reasons for this. First is the relative ease of transferring facilities from non-advanced or part-time work to meet the needs of full-time advanced students. Equally important is the remarkable method by which advanced further education is financed: it is rumoured that, when this was expounded to an incoming Secretary of State, he refused to believe it was true. The method is as follows. Expenditure is undertaken by individual local education authorities. At the end of the year the expenditure of all the local authorities is pooled, and the liability for it apportioned between authorities according to a formula based on school population and non-domestic rateable value. Thus, if one authority decides to increase its expenditure on advanced further education, it will, after the final reckoning, bear only a tiny part of the extra cost, most of which will be borne by other authorities which had no share in the original decision. The central government has to approve the establishment of every course, after taking advice from one of the Regional Advisory Councils on Further Education; but it has no specific power to control the scale at which the course is operated. It does have indirect influence through its right to approve expenditure on large items of equipment and through the pressures that can be exerted by Her Majesty's Inspectors. But broadly speaking there is little to discourage individual local authorities from expanding further education to the limits of students' demand for places. This is the mechanism whereby further education has come to play the role of safety valve.

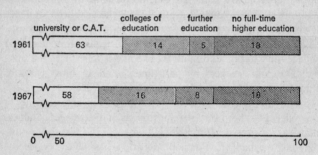

Figure 10.   Entrants to each sector having two or more A levels as a percentage of the output of those with two or more A levels, England and Wales[2]

The Robbins Committee cast it in this same role in the future, and since it envisaged a constant (and, later, rising) entry rate to universities and a rising entry rate to colleges of education, it recommended a slightly falling entry rate to further education. The formula was that the entry to further education should grow two-thirds as fast as A level output.

In the event, further education seems to have performed exactly the pre-assigned function of a safety valve, but the magnitudes have been quite different. This is best seen by looking back at Table 17. Since 1961 the university entry rate has fallen: the spillover has gone to colleges of education and to further education. But, whereas the intake into the colleges of education has been centrally planned – each college's intake is decided in negotiation with the D.E.S. – the expansion of further education is quantitatively unplanned. In this sense further education acts as a residual. But the outcome is noteworthy: the proportion of those with A levels who enter some form of full-time higher education is maintained more or less constant over time, even though the proportion going to university falls. This equilibrating mechanism, which was already in evidence up to 1961,[1] has continued to perform well ever since. To bring home the point, we have illustrated it in Figure 10.

In terms of numbers, further education in England and Wales doubled in the four years after 1962–3, while in Scotland the growth was more modest – in fact up to 1966–7 it was only as much as projected by Robbins. This is brought out in Table 19.

Table 19
Students in Full-time Advanced Further Education,
Great Britain (Thousands)

| | England and Wales | | Scotland | |
	Actual	Robbins	Actual	Robbins
1961–2	23·8	.	3·1	.
1962–3	28·0	.	3·1	.
1963–4	33·3	32·8	3·1	3·3
1964–5	39·6	35·7	3·6	3·7
1965–6	47·0	38·1	4·2	4·3
1966–7	54·5	40·4	4·7	4·6
1967–8	66·0	42·5	5·2	4·5

Which courses have expanded fastest? In England and Wales, as we should expect, it is the degree courses. In 1961–2 there were 5,500 students on these courses, if we include those leading to the Diploma in Technology (Dip. Tech.), most of which have now been converted to degree courses. Six years later, as Table 20 shows, the number had risen to just under 24,000. Higher National Diploma courses have also grown rapidly, while Art courses have been more or less static.

Table 20

Students in Full-time Advanced Further Education: by Type of Course, England and Wales

| | *Thousands* | | *Percentage growth* |
	1961–2	*1967–8*	
London degrees	4·2	13·7	226
C.N.A.A. degrees and Dip. Tech.	1·3	10·1	677
Higher National Diploma	4·0	14·2	255
National art qualifications	5·8	6·7	16
Professional qualifications, etc.	8·5	21·3	151
Total	23·8	66·0	177

The bald statistics of expansion do not reveal the equally important changes that have been happening in the content of courses in further education. In the 1950s a majority of the degree level work was on the traditional pattern, for London external and internal degrees. But in the last ten years a growing proportion of the courses, including all those for Dip.Tech. and many of those for Council for National Academic Award degrees, have been based on the 'sandwich' pattern. The idea is that by alternating between industry and college a student may see more clearly the relevance of his studies, while his teacher is forced to ensure that they actually are relevant. Great energy has been devoted to the design of these courses and the sandwich approach, previously available to only a few of our best-qualified young people, is now experienced by an increasingly large number. This book is not the place to discuss these curricular and institutional developments, but they are very important.[3]

For the future the polytechnics are planned as the centrepiece of advanced further education. If there are thirty of them with 2,000 full-timers each, they will provide 60,000 places – nearly as many as the total number of advanced full-time students now studying in very many more colleges. Whether it will be possible to concentrate together this number of students will of course depend on how many students there are altogether in the further education system. If, as some think, the polytechnics will be able to compete effectively with the universities – given sufficient money, and high enough salaries – there will be no problem. But, if the safety valve analogy remains broadly relevant, then the prospects for further education will depend on the relation between the future output of qualified school leavers, and the capacity of the universities.

Chapter Ten
Resources: Staff and Money

So far we have merely described the scale and pattern of expansion, without asking how it has been achieved. When the *Robbins Report* came out, *The Times* argued strongly that it would be impossible to staff the proposed expansion. The extra students might come forward, but they would inevitably be exposed to a falling quality of education. Not only staff but money for equipment, books and all the other necessary inputs would inevitably be subject to pinch-penny policies. The end might be willed, but the means would not be forthcoming.

This forecast has, on the whole, been proved wrong. Take teachers first. There is of course the vital question of quality, and we have to admit at once that we do not have any usable data on this. The U.G.C. do collect information on the qualifications of people recruited to university teaching but it is not published. It does seem to be fairly widely agreed, however, that in recent years it has been somewhat easier to get a university job than before, at least in the more rapidly growing subjects like the social sciences.[1] It is thus possible that there has been some falling off in quality, though our general impression is that universities have made strenuous efforts to guard their standards.

Meanwhile, the number of teachers has leapt upwards and, in both universities and colleges of education, seems to have kept pace with the growing number of students. In the universities, this is an inference rather than a statement of fact, and involves some niceties of definition. The problem arises because in 1965–6, the U.G.C. commendably introduced a better system of classifying university staff. The correct procedure in such cases is to collect information for the transitional year using both the old and the new definitions, so that the new time series can be spliced onto the old one. But, as often happens when statisticians improve their definitions, this was not done. Until 1965–6 universities were asked to record the number of 'full-time academic staff paid directly from university funds'. From 1965–6 onwards they were asked for the numbers of full-time staff 'who make a direct and significant contribution to the academic work (teaching and/or research) of the university and who would be regarded as properly belonging to the academic staff of the university, even if only temporarily'. These staff were divided into three categories: A those in posts financed *wholly* by the university (or college); B those in posts financed *in part* by the university (or college); and C others.

Table 21 shows the results of these inquiries for all universities, leaving out Oxford and Cambridge and the former C.A.T.s – for which the data are even weaker than for the other universities. For 1965–6 onwards it shows the results including Category A only and also including Categories A, B and C – the numbers in Category B are so small as not to be worth treating separately.

Table 21

University Teachers, Students and Staff/Student Ratio, Great Britain (Excluding Oxford, Cambridge and Former C.A.T.s)

	Full-time teachers	Full-time students	Students per teacher
1961–2	12,786	95,322	7·5
1962–3	13,801	101,136	7·3
1963–4	14,927	108,312	7·3
1964–5	16,774	119,681	7·1
1965–6 *Category A*	17,333	132,096	7·6
Categories A, B and C	20,373		6·5
1966–7 *Category A*	18,896	144,992	7·7
Categories A, B and C	22,310		6·5
1967–8 *Category A*	20,368	157,496	7·7
Categories A, B and C	24,108		6·5

Which of these two measures is the right one to compare with the figures for 1964–5 and earlier? The U.G.C. have used Category A only, as being the most comparable. This may or may not be right but the fact is that none of the measures is actually comparable. Scrutinize the table. It shows that the number of staff grew by over 1,000 in each year up to 1964–5 and by nearly 2,000 in that year. How much did it grow in the next year – the peak bulge year? It seems unlikely that it grew by less than 1,500.[2] But using Category A only we record an increase of 550, while using all categories we get 3,600. We ought therefore to include a substantial proportion of Categories B and C to get a valid comparison with earlier years.

For computing student/staff ratios we simply divide the number of students by the number of staff. This is not the method used by the U.G.C. which has been to count each postgraduate as equivalent to three undergraduates, except in the case of arts, where the Certificate of Education students were given a weighting of one and the others of two.[3] These weights are based on 'opinions gathered by the Committee' on the relative demands of undergraduates and postgraduates on staff time. In order, among other things, to get a more adequate impression of these demands, the U.G.C. asked the universities in their 1965–6 Returns to allocate expenditures according to the relative effort of the staff on undergraduate teaching, postgraduate teaching and research; in 1966–7 this was changed to the relative division of their time (rather than effort) between these three activities, and also administration. Presumably in due course the weightings will be altered to reflect the results of these inquiries. In the meantime, it seems best to rely on the results of the Robbins Committee's surveys which suggested that there was, in 1961–2, no appreciable difference in the demands of undergraduates and postgraduates on teachers' time.[4]

The simple ratios between full-time students and staff can be seen from Table 21. Between 1961–2 and 1964–5 there was a striking improvement, the ratio falling from 7·5 to 7·1. Put another way, the number of staff rose by 31 per cent, while students increased by 26 per cent. The student/staff ratio improved sharply in pure science and medicine, but worsened slightly in applied science. Then in 1965–6 came the new definitions. Including Category A staff only, the ratio worsened to 7·6; including all categories of staff it improved to 6·5. The broad impression is of no substantial change in 1965–6. Since then the position has been almost completely stable. As between faculties, there is since 1961–2 clear evidence of improvement in pure science and medicine, while in applied science the situation may have worsened somewhat (see Table 22).

In relation to the debate about strategies of expansion it is interesting to look at the student/staff ratio in the universities founded since 1960. It was 7·4, 6·9, 6·8, 7·8 and 8·5 in the years 1962–3 to 1966–7 (taking Category A only in the last two years). Such figures suggest that there are no overwhelming diseconomies in achieving expansion by the founding of new institutions. In the upgraded C.A.T.s the ratios in 1965–6 and 1966–7 were 6·6 and 7·0 – if anything less economical than the average of all universities, allowing for the predominance of technology in the former C.A.T.s.

In colleges of education, as in universities, the number of staff has grown closely in step with the number of students. In the year (1962–3) when the course was lengthened to three years, the student/staff ratio in England and Wales worsened from 10·1 to 11·1. But since then it has fallen slightly to 10·5 in 1967–8, despite the astonishing increase in the number of students. Altogether the number of staff more than doubled from 3,600 in 1961–2 to 9,100 in 1967–8. The people recruited came from a number of sources, but mainly from the schools.

The schools have also suffered from the rapid expansion of the teaching force in further education. Unfortunately there is no way of counting separately the numbers teaching advanced students in technical colleges without a survey of teaching arrangements like that carried out for Robbins. It is this kind of difficulty which makes further education, for statistical purposes, the 'darkest Africa' of the higher education system, and there is unfortunately no relevant information about it that we can use in this chapter.

We come now to the other resources used in universities and colleges of education. For teachers, though important, are not the only input, and the view of the Athenian general that 'Men not walls make a city' has never been the whole truth. At present teachers' salaries account for 37 per cent of the universities' current expenditures. If we include academic research staff, the figure is 44 per cent, while other wages and salaries amount to

Table 22

Full-time Students per Full-time Teacher in Universities: by Faculty, Great Britain (Excluding Oxford, Cambridge and Former C.A.T.s)

Ratio : 1

	Hum-anities	Social studies	All arts	Pure science	Applied science	Medi-cine	Agri-culture	All faculties
1938-9	..	..	11·0	4·9	7·3	28·0	4·8	10·2
1954-5	..	..	7·4	6·3	8·5	7·3	2·9	7·0
1961-2	8·8	9·0	8·8	7·2	8·2	6·0	3·0	7·5
1962-3	8·7	9·0	8·8	7·1	7·9	5·7	3·2	7·3
1963-4	8·5	9·1	8·6	7·1	8·1	5·5	3·0	7·3
1964-5	8·6	8·3	8·5	6·6	8·4	5·3	3·0	7·1
1965-6								
Category A	7·8*	10·5*	8·8	7·0	9·0	5·2	6·0	7·6
Categories A, B and C	..	..	..	..	..	..	..	6·5
1966-7								
Category A	8·0*	10·4*	8·9	7·0	8·6	5·3	6·2	7·7
Categories A, B and C	..	..	..	..	..	..	..	6·5

*The definitions differ from those in 1964-5 and earlier. 'Education' is included in humanities in all years.

another 20 per cent or more of expenditure. Other expensive items on the physical side are those connected with laboratory maintenance, and with the upkeep of buildings (see Table 23). Books and periodicals account for a very small proportion of the cost of universities, and in fact library staff cost as much.

Table 23
Breakdown of Current Expenditure in Universities, Great Britain, 1965–6

	£m.	Percentage
Salaries of teaching staff	58·8	37·0
Departmental maintenance		
Wages (technicians and lab. assistants)	16·2	10·2
Other (mainly equipment)	16·7	10·5
Libraries		
Wages and salaries	3·1	2·0
Books, periodicals, binding	3·2	2·0
Maintenance of buildings		
Wages of porters and maintenance staff	4·9	3·1
Repairs and maintenance (by outside staff)	6·7	4·2
Heat, light, water, rent and rates	10·8	6·8
Expenditure from research grants		
Salaries of academic staff	11·8	7·4
Other	6·7	4·2
Administration		
Salaries	7·2	4·5
Other	3·7	2·3
Other	9·1	5·7
Total	159·1	100·0

All of these figures prompt one to speculate about the possible savings to be obtained by spending more on one type of input and less on another – by substituting one for another. For example, could universities save by further substituting books for teachers, or even books for library staff? While posing the questions, the figures do not answer them.

They also remind us that one of the most controversial questions concerns the use of space. Could the universities educate students more cheaply if, as the colleges of education have been forced to do, they used the capital locked up in their buildings more intensively? The first approach to this question, as to the others we have asked, is to find out what proportion of costs are represented by the input in question. To measure the resource cost of buildings we need to know not the rate of capital expenditure on new buildings, but the value of the services currently rendered by all existing buildings, that is, their notional rent. The Robbins Committee estimated that buildings constituted 19 per cent of the resource cost of higher education as a whole, leaving aside the cost of students' time.[5] Thus if it were possible to cut down on building costs per student by, say, a quarter, without increasing other inputs, the total cost per student would fall by 5 per cent. By contrast, if the teacher cost per student could be cut by the same proportion, with no additional costs elsewhere, the overall saving would be nearly 10 per cent – because teachers represent 37 per cent of costs. If we stand back and make a dispassionate forecast, it seems likely that the main savings in resource costs of universities in the next decade or two will come through worsening of the student/staff ratio.[6] There are manifest economies of scale in universities, both in the use of libraries and equipment and in terms of teaching. Large lectures are as useful to the students who attend them as lectures given to smaller audiences. Thus, for example, Oxford and Cambridge, with their large lecture audiences, are able to run a system of intensive tutorial teaching, although their student/staff ratios are much worse than the national average. In future, universities will be larger than they are now and will be better able to reap these economies. But even if a worse staffing ratio were accompanied by no economies of scale, how serious would this be? The Robbins Committee found that in term time university teachers spend on average about seven and a half hours a week in contact with students.[7] They also found how the rest of their working time of forty hours a week was spent, and estimated that, if all of it was attributed to either teaching or research, the division of annual working time was about fifty-fifty.[8] This corresponded well with the results of various U.G.C. inquiries. So it is hard to believe that a, say, 10 per cent increase in teaching hours in term-time, if appropriately spread, would impose an intolerable burden; it would imply a less than 10 per cent reduction in research. The staffing ratio in Britain is higher than almost anywhere in the world, and current pressures towards greater productivity, especially if linked to extra pay, seem bound to produce some changes.[9]

But to revert to our original question. Has expansion been had on the cheap? Some universities have certainly done better than others, and there have been periods of nerve-racking uncertainty when the universities did not know their next year's allocations.[10] There have also been cuts and postponements of capital projects. But, taking a broad view of resource allocation, it does seem difficult to argue that the universities have had a poor financial deal during the period of the bulge, especially when they are compared with other parts of the educational system. As we explain in the next chapter, the prospects for the coming few years are much more gloomy, but here we are concerned with the past.

Between 1961–2 and 1966–7, universities' current expenditure rose from £74 million to £164 million at current prices – or to £184 million if we include the former colleges of advanced technology. These figures are distorted by price rises and to measure the change in real resources we need to deflate the figures in the top half of Table 24 by a price index which takes into account the detailed composition of university budgets.[11] The results appear in the bottom half of the table, which shows that the real resources going to universities (leaving out former C.A.T.s) increased by 75 per cent in the five years up to 1966–7.

But what about real resources per student? As Table 25 shows, these rose continuously so that by 1966–7 they were 23 per cent higher than five years earlier. In the years up to 1964–5 the data permit us to separate the improvement in teacher supply from other improvements.[12] They suggest that the teacher input per student increased by about 8 per cent; this compares well with the 5 per cent improvement in the student/staff ratio reported for those years earlier in the chapter. The main improvement was

Table 24

Current Expenditure in Universities, Great Britain

£
million

	Salaries of academic staff	Other	Total
At current prices			
Excluding former C.A.T.s			
1961–2	31·7	41·9	73·6
1962–3	35·8	48·8	84·6
1963–4	44·4	57·1	101·5
1964–5	53·6	67·8	121·4
1965–6	..	..	142·3
1966–7	..	..	163·7
Including former C.A.T.s			
1966–7	..	..	184·1
At constant (1961–2) prices			
Excluding former C.A.T.s			
1961–2	31·7	41·9	73·6
1962–3	32·3	47·1	79·4
1963–4	36·9	53·0	89·9
1964–5	41·4	60·0	101·4
1965–6	..	..	114·0
1966–7	..	..	128·4
Including former C.A.T.s			
1966–7	..	..	144·4

in the other inputs – equipment, ancillary staff and the like, where the improvement was about 19 per cent. It is of course quite right that the supplies of other inputs should rise relative to those of teachers, because teachers, and labour in general, are constantly getting more expensive relative to goods. Over the period covered by our data, it happens that the proportional rise in the ratio of other inputs to teachers was equal to the proportional rise in the relative price of teachers, so that academic

Table 25

Current Expenditure per Full-time Student in Universities, Great Britain (Excluding Former C.A.T.s)

£

	Salaries of academic staff	Other	Total
At current prices			
1961–2	259	342	601
1962–3	281	384	665
1963–4	330	424	754
1964–5	363	459	822
1965–6	..	..	885
1966–7	..	..	941
At constant (1961–2) prices			
1961–2	259	342	601
1962–3	254	374	624
1963–4	274	393	667
1964–5	280	406	686
1965–6	..	..	709
1966–7	..	..	738

salaries ended up forming the same proportion of total costs as they did at the beginning (43–44 per cent). The same is broadly true of the whole period since the First World War.[13]

We ought to stress that the absolute level of university expenditures per student is much higher than the true cost per student. The reason is that universities produce research as well as teaching, whereas by attributing all expenditures to students, we imply that teaching is the only output. One can attempt to separate out the research costs on the basis of the way staff time and other resources are allocated, but there are no standard time series on this. The best we can do over time is to compare the income obtained from research grants and contracts with total university expenditures: between 1961–2 and 1965–6 there was little change, the proportions being just over 11 per cent in each year. Thus, changes in total resources per student are likely to correspond broadly to teaching resources per student. We need not discuss whether rising inputs per student mean that productivity has declined, since it raises problems of measuring the educational and the research output of universities which are quite outside our scope.[14]

Over the period, universities' current expenditure rose from 0·30 per cent of the Gross National Product to 0·49 per cent – or 0·55 including former C.A.T.s. It also rose as a proportion of educational expenditure. As Vaizey has pointed out, this means that a rising share of educational outlays go on the children of the richer sections of the community.[15] And a growing proportion of university expenditure has been met by the central government, as other sources of income except fees are very inelastic. The U.G.C. grant rose from 70 to 74 per cent of the total current income of universities between 1961–2 and 1966–7.[16] And on top of this came the universities' capital expenditure, where the proportion of government finance was probably even higher.[17] Government capital expenditure rose from £29 million in 1961–2 to £71 million in 1966–7 – or £79 million including former C.A.T.s.[18] This latter figure approached the dimensions of the school building programme (£140 million in 1966). But the university outlays were of course exceptional and represent an accelerator effect connected with the atypical pace of expansion. In future years the capital programme will form a much smaller part of the government's total commitment to universities than the proportion of over a third in 1966–7. If we include the government's capital outlays with the total of current expenditure, the universities in that year absorbed 0·78 per cent of the whole national product.

In colleges of education current expenditure has risen even faster than in universities, but capital expenditure has not. In England and Wales current money outlays rose nearly two and a half times. The figures are shown in Table 26. They are not the ones we should ideally like because, as well as academic costs, they include the costs of board and lodging. So they cannot be used for comparing the absolute level of costs per student with those in universities; but they do give a reasonable picture of relative changes in costs per student over time.[19]

Between 1961–2 and 1966–7 university costs per student at current prices rose from £601 to £941 – by 57 per cent. The rise in colleges of education was much less – well below 20 per cent, and on top of this there were sharp economies in the provision of accommodation. It is interesting to compare these increases in cost per student with those of 32 per cent in primary schools, and 55 per cent in secondary. The pinch seems to have been felt equally in the primary schools and in the colleges where their teachers are taught, while the secondary schools and universities have done well by comparison.

Table 26

Current Expenditure in Colleges of Education, England and Wales

£ million

	Salaries of academic staff	Other wages and salaries	Other	Total
At current prices				
1961–2	6·3	3·6	7·4	17·3
1962–3	8·2	4·3	9·6	22·0
1963–4	9·8	5·1	11·0	25·9
1964–5	12·1	5·6	13·7	31·3
1965–6	15·5	6·8	16·3	38·5
1966–7	18·4	8·1	19·4	45·9
At constant (1961–2) prices				
1961–2	6·3	3·6	7·4	17·3
1962–3	7·9	4·1	9·4	21·4
1963–4	9·0	4·7	10·6	24·3
1964–5	10·7	5·0	12·6	28·3
1965–6	13·1	5·8	14·3	33·2
1966–7	15·0	6·6	16·4	38·0

In principle we should of course make each comparison in constant prices, but we lack a specific price index for college of education outlays.[20] If we deflate academic salaries by a general wage index, and other inputs by a general price index, we can get only a very rough idea of what has been happening. The results are in Table 27. They show, as the student/staff ratios

Table 27

Current Expenditure per Student in Colleges of Education, England and Wales

£

	Salaries of academic staff	Other wages and salaries	Other	Total
At current prices				
1961–2	173	99	203	474
1962–3	169	89	198	456
1963–4	179	93	201	473
1964–5	193	89	218	498
1965–6	212	93	222	525
1966–7	215	95	227	537
At constant (1961–2) prices				
1961–2	173	99	203	474
1962–3	163	85	194	442
1963–4	164	86	193	443
1964–5	170	80	201	451
1965–6	179	79	195	453
1966–7	175	77	192	444

showed, that the teacher input per student fell in 1962–3 but has since tended to recover. Non-teacher inputs per student seem on the whole to have fallen. As a result overall inputs per student have tended to fall. We should stress, however, that these estimates are based on very inadequate price indices and only the money costs per student are at all reliable.

While total current expenditures have risen sharply, total capital expenditures have been fairly stable.[21] At the beginning of the period they were already at a high level as a result of the programmes for raising the length of course and for going up to 80,000 places by 1970–1. As we have already explained, Mr Crosland's programme for raising student numbers by raising productivity involved only minor extra expenditure on the capital side, while the current expenditures were of course raised upwards.

In this chapter we have only touched on the broad patterns of expenditure on higher education. A complete analysis would have required a book on its own and we have only scratched the surface in order to get a general impression of what we might have found if we had gone deeper.

Chapter Eleven
The Future

The Robbins crash programme covered the years up to 1967–8. The period is over and the programme done. The years to come will be quite different and, from the point of view of expansion, much less hectic.

There is a common, but erroneous, impression that the reduced pace of expansion is due to the country's economic troubles. The universities' quinquennial settlement for the years up to 1971–2 provides for an increase of only about 25,000 students over the four years up to then, compared with an increase of 60,000 in the four years up to 1967–8. Although it preceded devaluation, this settlement has become connected in many people's minds with the devaluation cuts. In fact, however, it is meant to maintain university entry rates at the same level as over the last four years.[1] The reason why it is so low is quite simply the passing of the bulge.

As can be seen from Figure 11, the number of eighteen-year-olds reached its peak in 1965, and then began to fall. It will go on falling up to 1970 and will then stay in a trough till about 1974 when a steady rise will begin, corresponding to the increase in the birth rate from the mid-1950s onwards.

The trend is more uncertain. Figure 11 shows the latest published projection made by the Department of Education and Science.[2] According to this estimate the output of 'qualified school leavers' will be roughly constant over the five years 1967–71, the swelling 'trend' being just enough to offset the shrinking 'bulge'. From 1972 onwards the age groups will be constant and so the output of qualified school leavers will start rising, though at a sharper rate from the mid-70s when the age groups again start to increase.

The estimates are a good deal higher than those in the *Robbins Report*, as Table 28 shows. However, they do not seem un-

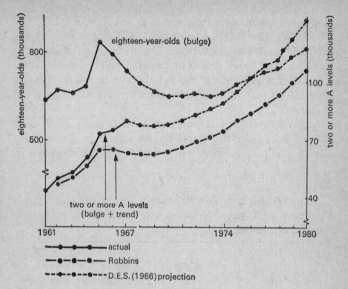

Figure 11. Number of eighteen-year-olds in June and number obtaining two or more A levels, England and Wales

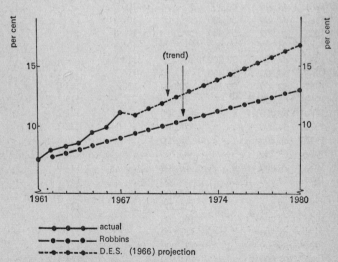

Figure 12. The percentage of the age group obtaining two or more A levels, England and Wales

reasonably high. In 1967 the actual A level output was 26 per cent higher than Robbins had predicted. The new forecasts for each year up to 1980 are between 19 and 26 per cent higher than Robbins. They do not predict that Robbins will be exceeded more in any future year than it has already been exceeded. This fact leads one to suspect, if anything, that the forecast is again too conservative.[3]

Suppose, however, that we accept it. What policy conclusions follow? To answer this would require another Robbins Committee. The first question would be the one we discussed in

Table 28

Output of Those with Two or More A Levels: Robbins Compared with Actual Numbers and D.E.S. (1966) Projection, England and Wales

	Robbins projection	Actual	D.E.S. (1966) projection	Actual as percentage of Robbins	D.E.S. (1966) projection as percentage of Robbins
1961	43,300	43,300	.	100·0	.
1962	47,400	50,800	.	107·2	.
1963	49,900	53,300	.	106·8	.
1964	56,500	60,600	.	107·3	.
1965	64,300	73,200	.	113·8	.
1966	64,700	75,400	.	116·5	.
1967	62,900	79,300	79,000	126·1	125·6
1968	61,900	.	77,800	.	125·7
1969	62,400	.	77,500	.	124·2
1970	64,000	.	78,300	.	122·3
1971	66,400	.	80,200	.	120·8
1972	68,700	.	83,200	.	121·1
1973	70,800	.	86,400	.	122·0
1974	74,600	.	89,600	.	120·1
1975	79,600	.	94,900	.	119·2
1976	84,200	.	101,900	.	121·0
1977	88,300	.	108,500	.	122·9
1978	93,300	.	115,000	.	123·3
1979	100,000	.	123,000	.	123·0
1980	105,800	.	131,600	.	124·4

chapter 2 – can plans really be based upon trends in the private demand for places? We argued that, even from a manpower point of view, this is not as bad a principle as it may appear. But even within it there would be many new considerations to be taken into account in making an effective plan. Instead we shall, purely for illustration, show for England and Wales how many places would be needed using the new A level forecast but otherwise following the Robbins assumptions. The rough answers are shown in Table 29[4] and the assumptions which they embody are, for universities:

(a) constant entry rate up to 1976, thereafter growing by 4 per cent per year simple interest till 1980;

(b) constant length of course;

(c) constant proportion of overseas students;

and for higher education as a whole:

(a) application rates constant, except for 10 per cent increase (at 2 per cent per year simple interest) from 1967 to 1972;

(b) constant acceptance rate;

(c) constant length of course;

(d) constant proportion of overseas students.

Table 29

Hypothetical 'Requirement' for Places Compared with Government Plans, England and Wales

		Universities	Colleges of education	Further education	Total
1971–2	Present plans	185,000	111,000	66,000	362,000
	Hypothetical requirement	205,000	.	.	382,000
1980–81	Hypothetical requirement	358,000	.	.	609,000

How do these figures compare with government plans? At present, these are no published plans for universities beyond 1971–2, nor for any sector beyond 1973–4. We will concentrate on 1971–2. At the time of writing, the Department of Education and

Science was engaged on the first comprehensive re-assessment of quantitative needs in higher education since Robbins, and the source for existing policy commitments are a variety of *ad hoc* statements some of which will doubtless be modified when new targets are announced.

For universities the Great Britain target is 220,000 – 225,000 places, as we have said, implying something like 185,000 in England and Wales. There have been suggestions that the universities will not be able to reach their targets for lack of money, but if this happens it will be for the first time in post-war history. The central government grant per student, according to the settlement, will rise from £754 to £775 over the quinquennium. By comparison with what has happened in the past this is a slender margin.[5] It is automatically protected against salary increases for teachers, but not against rising prices of other inputs. Moreover, as we said, the other sources of university income, except fees, are inelastic, and the grant will therefore have to provide for a rising proportion of expenditure per student. This may well set up downward pressure on the staff/student ratio, as it already has in some universities where staff who leave are not being replaced.

Would a worse staff/student ratio be a disaster? As we said earlier, in the long run it seems inevitable and, within reason, acceptable. But the phasing of these changes is also important. This seems to have got badly out of hand. During the last five years there have been enormous numbers of recruits to university teaching, drawn from relatively small cohorts of graduates. In the next five years, even with constant staffing ratios, fewer teachers will be recruited, and they will be drawn from much larger cohorts of graduates. University jobs will be much harder to get and the flow of graduates to industry and the schools enormously expanded. If on top of this the staffing ratio worsened, the number of recruits could become tiny. This could have very serious consequences. For in each generation there are some people who are clearly cut out by temperament and ability to be academics – others, many more in number, are marginal on one score or the other. For the long-term future of the universities it is vital that the first group should find university jobs. And, this apart, there are real risks to a profession whose age-structure is unbalanced – promotion blocks demoralize, while sudden improvements in prospects lift some people to posts above their stature, which a few years later demoralizes those below them. Thus in retrospect it would have been better if the staffing ratio had been allowed to get worse in the last five years and then improved in the next five. The Robbins Committee understandably did not recommend this course for fear that the former would happen but the latter would not. For the future, there is certainly no prospect of improved staffing ratios, but equally there is no reason to suppose that the U.G.C.'s targets for places will not be hit.

As we have said, this target will maintain present opportunities for qualified school leavers, but, as Table 29 makes clear, it is some 10 per cent too low to restore opportunities to the 1961 level recommended by Robbins. The target also falls short of that urged by the Committee of Vice-Chancellors and Principals on the basis of Robbins-type reasoning. That their recommendation was rejected is certainly connected with the binary philosophy of the Secretary of State who in effect rejected it.

In the rest of higher education, binarism has its expression in the government's target of 'over 60,000' places in further education in 1969–70[6] as compared with the Robbins target of 43,000 places. In fact there were already 66,000 students in 1967–8, and considerable expansion beyond this must be expected as the plan for polytechnics goes ahead, though current pressures on local authority finances will certainly restrain the rate of growth. Finally in teacher training we have the anomalous position that, although in 1967–8 the number of places was 20,000 above the Robbins target, the number planned for 1973–4 is still the same as in the *Robbins Report* (111,000). The number of entrants is already (at 35,000 in 1967) enough, if repeated in the next two years, to generate a student body of over 100,000 by 1969–70 and it is likely that considerable expansion will happen between then and 1973–4. However, nothing has been announced.

If we add together the 'planned' figures we have mentioned for the different sectors we get a total of 362,000 places in 1971–2 against 382,000 'required'. Thus current commitments are some 20,000 short of the overall Robbins-type requirement – the same as the shortfall on university places. An increased university programme would therefore kill two birds with one stone, but official aims lean towards increased programmes in the other sectors. For the longer term, government plans are still unformed, but it is vital to remember that, whereas the early 1970s are a period of relatively slowly growing demand, the middle 1970s will feel the full effects of the A level upsurge that is bound to come; and at least 600,000 places in full-time higher education may be needed in England and Wales alone by 1980. Hopefully, as the Robbins Committee recommended, the government will produce and publish regular plans for a period of ten years ahead, in order that we are never again caught napping, as we so nearly were in the mid-1960s. An important aspect of this is that the government should issue an annual series bringing the key tables in the *Robbins Report* and its Appendixes up to date, as we have tried in a limited way to do in this book.

What does all this mean for the average sixth-former hoping for higher education? In the next few years entry to universities will be about as difficult as it is now, though it may become easier in science subjects and harder in arts. Access to colleges of education and to further education is not likely to become any harder than at present. In the longer term, entry will become more difficult, to universities at any rate, unless plans are rapidly set in motion to meet the bulge of the 1970s.

The immediate future will thus resemble the immediate past, in terms of opportunities for qualified school leavers. Since 1962, despite the enormous increase in the number of students, it has not become any easier for people with good school leaving qualifications to enter university. But equally, despite the population bulge, it has not become more difficult. The *Robbins Report* played an important part in securing this. Its targets have been fully met in universities, and greatly exceeded in the colleges of education and in further education. This only points the moral that greater changes are often possible than seem likely in prospect, and the changes of the future will surprise even the expansionists of today.

Chapter Notes

Chapter 1

1. For definitions of higher education, universities, colleges of education, further education and so on, see Appendix D. Throughout the book, unless otherwise stated, universities include the former colleges of advanced technology (C.A.T.s) in all years, even though they only became universities in name in 1965. For sources to tables and figures, see Appendix B, and for sources to statistics in the text, see Appendix C. Appendix A contains a series of useful tables which would have encumbered the main text.

2. In these figures the former colleges of advanced technology, which only became universities in 1965, are included as universities in all years, as they are throughout this book unless otherwise stated; but if we exclude them the proportion fell by a similar amount – from 73 to 59 per cent.

3. *Higher Education. Report of the Committee appointed by the Prime Minister under the Chairmanship of Lord Robbins 1961–63*, H.M.S.O., 1963, Cmnd 2154.

4. For a discussion of the qualitative as well as quantitative recommendations of the *Report*, and of their implementation, see Lord Robbins, *The University in the Modern World*, Macmillan, 1966, especially chapter 8. A record of the main events can be found in the relevant chapters of the Annual Reports of the Department of Education and Science, and the Annual Surveys and Quinquennial Reports of the University Grants Committee.

5. The chapters of the *Report* which are the most relevant background to this book are chapters 6, 11 and 18.

6. *Higher Education. Government Statement on the Report of the Committee under the Chairmanship of Lord Robbins, 1961–63*, H.M.S.O., 1963, Cmnd 2165.

7. It is also relevant that the Robbins figures for 1973–4 were not a great deal higher than for 1967–8, as the latter were swollen by the 'bulge'. This undoubtedly made the government more willing to enter into a ten-year commitment than it might otherwise have been.

8. In 1967, for the first time, the number of university entrants significantly exceeded the Robbins target (see Figure 5), but by much less, proportionately, than the A level output exceeded the Robbins prediction.

Chapter 2

1. *The Times*, 28 October 1963.

2. See *The Times*, Leaders of 28 September and 5 October 1964, and letters from C. A. Moser and P. R. G. Layard of 29 September and 8 October 1964.

3. *Appendix One*, p. 97.

4. See J. Floud, 'The Robbins Report and the reform of higher education', in *The World Year Book of Education, 1967, Educational Planning*, ed. G. Z. F. Bereday, J. A. Lauwerys and M. Blaug, Evans Brothers Ltd, 1967.

5. For a discussion of these methods, see C. A. Moser and P. R. G. Layard, 'Planning the Scale of Higher Education: Some Statistical Problems', *J.R.S.S.* Series A, 4, 1964, reprinted in M. Blaug (ed.), *Economics of Education I*, Penguin Books, 1968. Blaug's book of Readings also contains many useful articles on this general topic. For a general bibliography see M. Blaug, *Economics of Education: A Selected Annotated Bibliography*, Pergamon Press, 1966.

6. The social rate of return depends on the pre-tax income differential between people with and without higher education, and on the social cost of higher education. The private rate of return depends on the above, together with the rates of taxation and the rates of subsidization of higher education. Thus the absolute levels of private and social rates of return differ. But suppose that the demand for educated people, viewed as a function of their relative wages, grows at a given rate, that proportional tax rates are constant and that social costs and subsidies rise at the same rate as average wages per head. Then the shift in supply of educated people needed to keep the social rate of return constant will also maintain the private rate of return at its present level. All of this assumes, of course, that external economies and diseconomies are negligible, or constant in importance.

7. For the influence of student grants on private demand, see *Report*, para. 645 and *Appendix One*, p. 100, para. 15.

8. See B. Thwaites in Association of Commonwealth Universities, *Home Universities Conference, 1963, Report of Proceedings*, A.C.U., London, 1963, p. 68.

Chapter 3

1. Throughout the chapter we deal mainly with the numbers getting two or more A levels. Fortunately, it happens that since 1961 the ratio between the numbers getting one, two and three or more A levels has been practically constant. For example, in 1966, 6·0 per cent of the age group got three or more A levels, 3·6 per cent got two A levels and 3·2 per cent got one only. It is this ratio of 60:36:32 which has been almost constant and so we get an adequate impression of A level trends by concentrating on only one measurement, such as 'two or more A levels.'

2. *Report*, paras. 167–71.

3. 11 per cent is 0·58 (from Table 5) as a percentage of 5·1 (from Table 4) – and similarly for boys.

4. The 'actual' average increments for two or more A levels in 1961–7 exaggerate the underlying trend, and the average annual increments calculated by least squares regression are boys: 0·66; girls: 0·50; boys and girls: 0·61.

5. *Appendix One*, part II and part IV, pp. 99–102.

6. See for example the 'Coleman Report', J. S. Coleman *et al.*, *Equality of Educational Opportunity*, U.S. Department of Health, Education and Welfare, Office of Education, 1966; J. W. B. Douglas *et al.*, *All Our Future: A Longitudinal Study of Secondary Education*, Peter Davies, 1968; and S. Wiseman, *Education and Environment*, Manchester University Press, 1964.

7. In America, R. Campbell and B. N. Siegel, 'The demand for higher education in the United States, 1919–64', *American Economic Review*, June 1967, represents a preliminary attempt, which fails, however, to determine the separate affects of G.N.P. in raising the investment and consumption demands for education.

8. See Appendix A, Table A.5 below.

9. If there is any better method now available than linear extrapolation of trends over an arbitrarily selected number of recent years, it would seem to lie in a compromise between the straight line and exponential models, for example in one based on a moving average. We considered the use of a moving average increment that rises linearly with time. It happens that if a five-year moving average had been put to the data for 1954–61 and extrapolated to 1966 it would have given a good prediction.

10. See Appendix A, Table A.5 below.

11. Abnormally large age groups of course face a poor market situation at whatever stage they complete their education; and it might be argued that this leads people to stay on longer in order to escape the unfavourable prospects for those who leave early. But staying on still involves substantial costs which will only be undertaken if substantial benefits are expected.

12. *Appendix One*, Annex R.

13. *Appendix One*, p. 113.

14. We hope to report on this in a separate article.

15. By home students we mean those ordinarily resident in the United Kingdom apart from their period as students.

Chapter 4

1. See *Hansard*, 27 October 1967, cols. 591–2.

2. The 1963 and 1964 data here exclude applicants to former C.A.T.s only, and the 1965 data include them. This suggests that in 1963 and 1964 most of those who applied to C.A.T.s also applied to universities. There is one qualification to this: even in 1965 there were a large number of C.A.T. applicants who did not apply through U.C.C.A., and presumably their counterparts in earlier years did not apply to universities.

3. The observant reader will ask why 62 per cent of 77 per cent is not equal to 58 per cent (the entry rate in Table 1). The reason is that 62 per cent relates to the percentage of those applying, whether for the first time or not, who are accepted. Seventy-seven per cent relates to those applying for the first time. An applicant's chance of ultimate success exceeds 62 per cent: it is 75 per cent (58 per cent divided by 77 per cent).

Chapter 5

1. For a fuller analysis of the swing, see Council for Scientific Policy, *Enquiry into the Flow of Candidates in Science and Technology into Higher Education*, H.M.S.O., 1968, Cmnd 3541 (the *Dainton Report*). See also C. M. Phillips, *Changes in Subject Choice at School and University*, Weidenfeld and Nicolson, 1969.

2. Most of this increase has probably been in social studies, but because of changes in definitions we cannot be precise about this.

3. On the issues discussed below see also Moser and Layard, op. cit., pp. 510–11 (reprinted in M. Blaug, ed., op. cit., pp. 313–15.)

4. University Grants Committee, *Annual Survey, Academic Year 1966–67*, H.M.S.O., 1968, Cmnd 3510, Appendix C.

5. *Dainton Report*, op. cit., para. 5.

6. A follow-up study of a sample of graduates from the 1966 Sample Census currently being undertaken on behalf of the Department of Education and Science will help here.

7. The case of doctors is different and their high pay helps to explain the still strong demand to study medicine. In addition, there is the explanation given in the *Dainton Report* that the subject is less 'out of touch with human and social affairs' (para. 151), but this was equally true in the 1950s.

8. There are of course techniques of producing some variation (e.g. responsibility allowances in schools, accelerated promotion). See for example W. G. Bowen, 'University salaries: faculty differentials', *Economica*, November 1963. Fortunately the Swann Committee have now recommended the introduction of explicit subject differentials in schools, but this will be strongly opposed by the teachers. See Committee on Manpower Resources

for Science and Technology, *The Flow into Employment of Scientists, Engineers and Technologists*, Report of the Working Group on Manpower for Scientific Growth (the *Swann Report*), H.M.S.O., 1968, Cmnd 3760, p. 69, para. 137.

9. For example, if we consider 1965 home entrants with three A levels, 23 per cent of those in pure science had an average grade better than B, compared with only 13 per cent in Applied Science (U.C.C.A. institutions only).

10. *Robbins Report*, p. 77, para. 204.

11. *Swann Report*, op. cit., p. 92, para. 13.

12. The debate about sixth-form specialization has been proceeding actively for ten years since the *Crowther Report* recommended a watered-down education in numeracy for sixth-formers. The first person to make really radical proposals, of the kind now becoming almost orthodox, was A. D. C. Peterson whose pamphlet, *Arts and Science Sides in the Sixth Form*, A Report to the Gulbenkian Foundation, Oxford University Department of Education, 1960, is still as relevant as it was then.

13. *The Times*, 25 September 1968.

Chapter 6

1. *Robbins Report*, p. 101, para. 293.

2. The figures for graduate output include overseas students, but the proportion here is small, and the fall in this proportion does not significantly affect the result. The table excludes former C.A.T.s.

3. These remarks relate to England and Wales excluding C.A.T.s, see Appendix A, Table A.10 below. In Scotland and in C.A.T.s the fluctuations were greater but there was no clear trend up or down.

4. See *Robbins Report, Appendix Two (A)*, pp. 127, 132, and University Grants Committee, *Enquiry into Student Progress, 1968*, H.M.S.O., 1968, especially para. 57.

5. Royal Commission on Medical Education, 1965–68, *Report*, H.M.S.O., 1968, Cmnd 3569.

6. Here 97 per cent do courses – mostly the Postgraduate Certificate of Education.

7. The table excludes former C.A.T.s and postgraduates on courses of teacher training. Including the teacher training students, the overall proportion of postgraduates rose from 17·5 in 1962–3 to 18·4 per cent in 1966–7.

8. See note 4, chapter 5.

9. The figures corresponding to the bottom row but including former C.A.T.s were: 7,610, 9,150, 16,760 , 5·0, 2·6, 9·1.

Chapter 7

1. This decision became effective on 1 April 1964.

2. The decision was announced in the House of Commons on 11 December 1964. In fairness it should be said that many of the universities had attached conditions to their offers of marriage.

3. The speech was given on 27 April 1965. Mr Crosland had been faced with requests from many of the regional technical colleges – that they should either join existing universities, or become universities themselves. He decided to reject these requests, his aim being to prevent the colleges abandoning their lower level work. At the same time he held out to them the prospect of developing to a very high level the more advanced of the work they were already doing.

4. For the Robbins Committee's arguments in favour of a central role for the universities see the *Robbins Report*, pp. 150–52 and 117–21. In practical terms the consequences of these arguments were more effectively worked out in relation to teacher training than to further education. For a powerful exposition of the opposite case see Eric E. Robinson, *The New Polytechnics*, Penguin Books, 1968.

5. See Department of Education and Science, *A Plan for Polytechnics and Other Colleges*, H.M.S.O., 1966, Cmnd 3006. A crucial test of whether the policy is being implemented fully will be whether teachers in polytechnics are paid at university salary levels.

Chapter 8

1. The plan was for 80,000 places in 'general' and 'specialist' colleges. If all colleges are included (technical teacher training colleges as well) about 82,000 places were implied.

2. See National Advisory Council on the Training and Supply of Teachers. *Ninth Report, The Demand for and Supply of Teachers, 1963–1986*, H.M.S.O., 1965.

3. See College Letter, No. 7/65, of 3 July 1965, following Mr Crosland's speech to the National Union of Teachers at Douglas in April 1965.

4. The column headed 'No full-time higher education' is simply a residual. In Table 1 all entrants to former C.A.T.s were treated as having two or more A levels. Here, more realistically, we allow for their changing pattern of qualifications, but the effective difference is small.

Chapter 9

1. See *Robbins Report, Appendix One*, p. 126, Table 20.

2. See note 4 to chapter 8.

3. For a discussion of these types of courses see Robinson, op. cit., and a forthcoming book on the colleges of advanced technology by T. Burgess and J. Pratt, to be published by Allen Lane The Penguin Press.

Chapter 10

1. There has been no significant change in the distribution of university staff between grades, but this unfortunately cannot be used to make any inference about the quality of university staff.

2. Further evidence on this comes from expenditure per student on p. 85.

3. U.G.C. *Returns 1960–61*, paras. 37–45.

4. See *Appendix Three*, pp. 80–83. A similar result for social studies was obtained, by more rigorous methods, for teaching at the London School of Economics in 1964–5. See H. Glennerster, *Graduate School: A Study of Graduate Work at the London School of Economics*, Oliver and Boyd, 1966.

5. *Appendix Four*, p. 153, Table E.2. In 1962–3 current expenditure on teaching and research was £123 million and the imputed rent of buildings, etc., £28 million.

6. There are also likely to be budgetary savings in student maintenance grants through some scheme of income-related repayment, but these grants are transfer expenditures and not resource costs.

7. *Appendix Three*, p. 56, Table 60.

8. ibid., p. 66, Table 66.

9. These are vividly described and analysed in the Annual Reports of the Principal of the University of London.

10. The above was written before the P.I.B. report on university pay, National Board for Prices and Incomes, *Standing Reference on the Pay of University Teachers in Great Britain, First Report*, Report No. 98, H.M.S.O., Cmnd 3866, 1968. It seems even more plausible in the light of this report.

11. A different approach, with a different purpose, is to deflate university expenditures by a general price index of all goods and services in the economy. Since the prices of university inputs, especially teachers, have risen faster than the general price index, this method estimates a more rapid increase in the real cost of universities than the increase in real inputs shown in Table 24. The reason is simple: the inputs are now being measured not in their own units, but in units of what they could produce elsewhere in the economy; and each year the alternative product of most university inputs, especially teachers, rises.

12. The definition of academic salaries used up to 1964–5 does not seem to be the same as the sum of teachers salaries and salaries met from research grants shown in Table 23 for 1965–6.

13. J. Vaizey and J. Sheehan, *Resources for Education*, George Allen and Unwin 1968, p. 125. This volume contains a fuller discussion of many of the topics treated in the present chapter. It is interesting to note that in primary and secondary schools teachers' salaries have formed a declining proportion of total costs – the relative rise in salaries being accompanied by a more than proportionate increase in non-teacher inputs (op. cit., pp. 53, 56, 61 and 152).

14. On these questions see M. Woodhall and M. Blaug, 'Productivity Trends in British University Education', *Minerva*, Summer 1965.

15. Vaizey and Sheehan, op. cit., p. 137.

16. This remark excludes former C.A.T.s.

17. There are no data on privately financed capital expenditure in this period.

18. See Appendix A, Table A.12 below.

19. In 1966–7, board and lodging amounted to £14·8 million out of a total expenditure of £45·9 million. It is possible that the proportion of expenditure going on tuition has risen somewhat over time, in which case the figures in the next paragraph somewhat understate the percentage increase in tuition expenditure per student.

20. It is highly desirable that official indices of input prices should be regularly published for each level of education.

21. See Appendix A, Table A.13 below.

Chapter 11

1. The numbers who obtained two or more A levels in the four years 1964–7 were 288,000 and the projected numbers (see Table 28) for the four years 1968–71 is 314,000 – an increase of only 9 per cent. Planned places will rise from 200,000 in 1967–8 to between 220,000 and 225,000 in 1971–2 an increase of between 10 and 12½ per cent.

2. *Statistics of Education, 1966*, vol. 2, pp. xxii–xxv and Table 26. This is based on data up to 1966 only. A revised projection, of staying at school only, is now available based on 1967 data; this forecasts, for example, that the number of seventeen-year-olds in school in 1970 will be 4 per cent higher than in the 1966 forecast (see *Statistics of Education, 1967*, vol. 1, Table 43).

3. Against this, the 'trend' seems to have been extrapolated in a linear fashion. We have not been able to explain why the difference between the new projections and Robbins is proportionately greater in Figure 12 than in Figure 11.

4. The method of calculation was only approximate. The Robbins projection of places in academic year X was multiplied in each case by the ratio of the latest estimate of A level output in academic year $(X—2)$ to the

Robbins estimate of the same output. For universities we used the output of two or more A levels and for all higher education the output of one or more A levels.

5. There will also be severe difficulties on the capital side in some universities, as a result of the recent (Summer 1968) letter from the Chairman of the U.G.C. to vice-chancellors announcing substantial delays in the building programme.

6. See D.E.S., *A Plan for Polytechnics and Other Colleges*, op. cit., para. 9.

Appendix A
Further Tables

Readers may find it helpful to have in a more complete form some of the time series referred to in the text. This Appendix provides a number of the more important of these. Notes to these tables appear on page 121 and their sources on pages 132–8.

Table A.1

Number of Eighteen-year-olds in June and the Percentage Obtaining Two or More A Levels, England and Wales

	Eighteen-year-olds (Thousands)		Numbers obtaining two or more A levels (Thousands)		Percentage of age group obtaining two or more A levels	
	Actual	Robbins	Actual	Robbins	Actual	Robbins
1954	561	•	24·6	•	4.3	•
1955	566	•.	25·6	•	4·5	•
1956	577	•	27·3	•	4·8	•
1957	577	•	29·9	•	5·3	•
1958	563	•	31·9	•	5·7	•
1959	532	•	34·0	•	6·2	•
1960	572	•	38·1	•	6·6	•
1961	637	•	43·3	•	6·9	•
1962	672	675	50·8	47·4	7·6	7·2
1963	660	665	53·3	49·9	8·0	7·5
1964	684	671	60·6	56·5	8·3	7·8
1965	835	863	73·2	64·3	9·2	8·1
1966	790	773	75·4	64·7	9·6	8·4
1967	730	718	79·3	62·9	10·9	8·8

Table A.2

Number of Eighteen-year-olds in June and the Percentage
Obtaining Two or More A Levels, England and Wales

| | Eighteen-year-olds (Thousands) | | Numbers obtaining two or more A levels (Thousands) | | Percentage of age group obtaining two or more A levels | |
	D.E.S. 1966	Robbins	D.E.S. 1966	Robbins	D.E.S. 1966	Robbins
1967	728	718	79·0	62·9	10·2	8·8
1968	695	685	77·8	61·9	10·7	9·1
1969	665	664	77·5	62·4	11·3	9·4
1970	648	647	78·3	64·0	11·8	9·8
1971	652	660	80·2	66·4	12·3	10·1
1972	660	664	83·2	68·7	12·7	10·4
1973	650	650	86·4	70·8	13·2	10·8
1974	664	672	89·6	74·6	13·7	11·0
1975	690	698	94·9	79·6	14·2	11·4
1976	719	721	101·9	84·2	14·6	11·7
1977	734	742	108·5	88·3	15·1	12·0
1978	748	750	115·0	93·3	15·7	12·3
1979	785	787	123·0	100·0	16·2	12·6
1980	817	809	131·6	105·8	16·7	12·9

Table A.3

Total Output of Those with O and A Level Passes as Percentage of the Age Group, England and Wales

		Three or more A levels	Two or more A levels	One or more A levels	Five or more O levels
Boys					
Actual	1961	5·9	8·7	10·8	16·1
	1962	6·6	9·5	11·7	16·1
	1963	6·9	9·8	12·4	17·0
	1964	7·1	10·3	13·0	18·0
	1965	7·5	11·2	14·1	18·8
	1966	7·8	11·6	14·8	18·6
	1967	8·6	13·0	16·6	18·9
Robbins 1967		*7·6*	*11·2*	*13·9*	*20·2*
Girls					
Actual	1961	2·9	5·1	7·3	15·4
	1962	3·4	5·6	8·0	15·7
	1963	3·3	5·8	8·4	15·7
	1964	3·6	6·2	8·8	16·5
	1965	4·1	7·1	10·1	17·8
	1966	4·1	7·5	10·8	17·6
	1967	5·1	8·6	12·4	18·0
Robbins 1967		*3·6*	*6·3*	*9·1*	*18·6*
Boys and girls					
Actual	1961	4·4	6·9	9·1	15·8
	1962	5·0	7·6	9·9	15·9
	1963	5·1	8·0	10·4	16·4
	1964	5·4	8·3	10·9	17·1
	1965	5·9	9·2	12·2	18·3
	1966	6·0	9·6	12·8	18·1
	1967	6·9	10·9	14·6	18·6
Robbins 1967		*5·6*	*8·8*	*11·5*	*19·6*

Table A.4

Percentage of Each Age Group at School in January, England and Wales

	Nineteen and over		Eighteen		Seventeen		Sixteen		Fifteen	
	Actual	Robbins	Actual	Robbins	Actual	Robbins	Actual	Robbins	Actual	Robbins
Boys										
1958	0·6	·	4·5	·	11·1	·	20·0	·	37·4	·
1959	0·6	·	4·9	·	11·5	·	21·6	·	39·4	·
1960	0·7	·	4·9	·	12·4	·	22·6	·	40·8	·
1961	0·6	·	5·1	·	13·1	·	23·0	·	41·0	·
1962	0·6	·	5·4	·	13·4	·	23·2	·	43·5	·
1963	0·7	0·7	5·5	5·7	13·8	14·1	25·6	25·3	45·7	44·5
1964	0·6	0·7	5·4	5·9	14·9	15·1	26·4	25·9	59·2	63·3
1965	0·6	0·8	6·0	6·3	15·3	15·5	27·8	26·8	60·9	64·7
1966	0·7	0·8	6·0	6·5	16·2	16·2	29·2	27·7	63·7	65·6
1967	0·7	0·8	6·5	6·8	17·4	16·8	30·9	28·7	66·0	66·5

Girls

1958	0·2	·	2·3	·	8·8	·	18·5	·	35·7	·
1959	0·2	·	2·4	·	9·1	·	19·7	·	37·3	·
1960	0·2	·	2·5	·	9·7	·	20·4	·	38·7	·
1961	0·2	·	2·7	·	10·2	·	20·9	·	39·0	·
1962	0·2	·	2·8	·	10·4	·	20·7	·	41·2	·
1963	0·3	0·2	3·0	3·0	10·6	10·8	23·0	22·6	43·0	41·7
1964	0·2	0·2	3·0	3·1	11·6	11·5	23·4	23·0	58·6	61·2
1965	0·2	0·2	3·5	3·3	12·2	11·8	25·1	23·6	61·4	62·3
1966	0·2	0·2	3·6	3·4	13·2	12·2	27·1	24·3	63·5	63·1
1967	0·2	0·2	4·0	3·5	14·6	12·6	28·8	25·0	65·3	63·7

Boys and girls

1958	0·4	·	3·5	·	10·1	·	19·3	·	36·6	·
1959	0·4	·	3·7	·	10·3	·	20·7	·	38·4	·
1960	0·4	·	3·7	·	11·1	·	21·5	·	39·8	·
1961	0·4	·	3·9	·	11·7	·	22·0	·	40·0	·
1962	0·4	·	4·1	·	11·9	·	21·9	·	42·3	·
1963	0·5	0·5	4·3	4·3	12·2	12·5	24·4	24·0	44·4	43·1
1964	0·4	0·5	4·2	4·5	13·3	13·3	24·9	24·6	58·9	62·3
1965	0·4	0·5	4·8	4·8	13·8	13·7	26·4	25·3	61·5	63·6
1966	0·5	0·5	4·8	5·0	14·7	14·2	28·2	26·1	63·7	64·4
1967	0·5	0·5	5·3	5·2	16·0	14·8	29·9	26·9	65·6	65·2

Table A.5

Annual Increments in Staying at School, A Level Performance and G.N.P., England and Wales

	Percentage of children at school in January of year X minus percentage in year (X–1)			Percentage of the age group obtaining two or more A levels in year X minus percentage in year (X–1)	G.N.P. (at 1958 prices) in year (X–1) minus G.N.P. in year (X–2) (Index No.)
Year X	Fifteen-year-olds	Sixteen-year-olds	Seventeen-year-olds		
1955	1·2	1·1	0·3	0·2	3·5
1956	1·2	0·8	0·6	0·2	2·5
1957	1·2	1·0	0·5	0·5	2·2
1958	1·5	0·6	0·8	0·4	2·0
1959	1·8	1·4	0·3	0·5	—
1960	1·4	0·8	0·8	0·4	3·3
1961	0·2	0·5	0·5	0·3	5·0
1962	2·3	–0·1	0·3	0·7	4·0
1963	2·1	2·5	0·3	0·4	1·5
1964	14·5	0·5	1·1	0·3	4·8
1965	2·6	1·5	0·5	0·9	6·8
1966	2·2	1·8	0·9	0·4	3·4
1967	1·9	1·7	1·3	1·3	1·6

Table A.6

Net Output from Further Education of Those with A Level Passes, England and Wales

	Three or more A levels		Two or more A levels		One or more A levels	
	Actual	Robbins	Actual	Robbins	Actual	Robbins
Boys						
1961	1,000	.	1,800	.	3,200	.
1962	1,500	.	2,300	.	4,200	.
1963	1,600	1,200	2,800	2,100	5,200	3,800
1964	1,800	1,300	3,200	2,300	5,700	4,100
1965	2,100	1,400	3,600	2,500	6,900	4,400
1966	2,300	1,500	4,300	2,600	8,000	4,700
1967	2,800	1,600	5,200	2,800	9,400	5,000
Girls						
1961	300	.	700	.	1,800	.
1962	400	.	800	.	2,600	.
1963	700	400	1,100	800	3,000	2,100
1964	700	400	1,200	900	3,600	2,300
1965	700	400	1,600	1,000	4,500	2,500
1966	800	500	1,900	1,000	5,600	2,600
1967	1,200	500	2,500	1,100	6,600	2,800
Boys and girls						
1961	1,300	.	2,500	.	5,000	.
1962	1,900	.	3,100	.	6,800	.
1963	2,300	1,600	3,800	2,900	8,200	5,900
1964	2,500	1,700	4,400	3,200	9,300	6,400
1965	2,800	1,800	5,200	3,500	11,400	6,900
1966	3,100	1,900	6,200	3,600	13,600	7,300
1967	3,900	2,000	7,700	3,800	16,100	7,700

Table A.7

Home Initial Entrants to Universities as Percentage of Those with Two or More A Level Passes: by Subject,[1] Entrants from England and Wales

	Percentage of those qualified in arts subjects reading			Percentage of those qualified in science subjects reading					Percentage of all qualified entering
	Humanities	Social studies	Total	Pure science	Applied science	Medicine	Agriculture	Total	
Men									
Excluding former C.A.T.s									
1961	41	24	64	30	22	11	3	66	65
1962	36	22	58	28	19	10	3	59	59
1963	35	22	56	27	19	10	2	59	58
1964	33	23	56	27	18	10	2	58	57
1965	27*	26*	53	28	18	9	2	57	55
1966	25*	25*	50	29	19	9	2	59	55
Including former C.A.T.s									
1965	27*	28*	55	31	32	9	2	73	66
1966	26*	27*	53	32	33	9	2	77	65

Women									
Excluding former C.A.T.s									
1961	35	8	43	41	2	14	2	59	48
1962	30	8	38	37	2	12	2	54	42
1963	31	8	39	38	2	12	1	53	43
1964	31	8	39	36	1	11	2	49	42
1965	27*	13*	39	35	3	8	2	47	42
1966	25*	13*	38	37	4	10	2	52	42
Including former C.A.T.s									
1965	27*	13*	41	37	6	8	2	52	44
1966	26*	14*	39	39	6	10	2	58	44
Men and women									
Excluding former C.A.T.s									
1961	38	16	54	32	18	12	3	65	59
1962	33	15	48	30	15	11	3	58	53
1963	33	15	47	30	15	11	2	58	52
1964	32	15	48	29	15	10	2	56	52
1965	27*	20*	46	29	15	8	2	55	50
1966	25*	19*	44	30	16	9	2	58	50
Including former C.A.T.s									
1965	27*	21*	48	32	26	8	2	68	57
1966	26*	20*	46	34	27	10	2	72	57

Table A.8

Home Initial Entrants to Full-time Higher Education from England and Wales

	Universities (excl. former C.A.T.s)	Former C.A.T.s	Colleges of education	Further education	All full-time higher education
Men					
1961	18,070	2,420	4,870	5,800	31,150
1962	18,930	3,000	5,080	7,160	34,160
1963	19,720	3,270	6,330	8,440	37,770
1964	21,810	3,900	7,130	10,140	42,980
1965	25,160	4,680	8,290	11,940	50,070
1966	25,710	4,860	9,350	13,960	53,880
1967	27,410	5,190	9,540	17,320	59,460
Women					
1961	7,520	250	11,460	1,740	20,960
1962	7,900	330	12,390	2,280	22,900
1963	8,250	380	14,980	3,070	26,670
1964	9,450	490	17,310	3,310	30,570
1965	11,560	580	21,150	3,650	36,940
1966	12,020	640	23,950	4,280	40,890
1967	12,650	760	25,190	5,980	44,580
Men and women					
1961	25,580	2,670	16,320	7,540	52,110
1962	26,820	3,330	17,470	9,440	57,060
1963	27,960	3,650	21,310	11,520	64,440
1964	31,250	4,390	24,440	13,460	73,550
1965	36,720	5,260	29,450	15,590	87,010
1966	37,730	5,500	33,300	18,240	94,780
1967	40,060	5,950	34,740	23,300	104,040

Table A.9 appears on pp. 118–19.

Table A.10

Length of Course[2] in Universities (Excluding Former C.A.T.s),[3] Great Britain

	Home initial entrants	Home under-graduates	Home post-graduates	Under-graduate length of course (Years)	Postgraduates as percentage of entrants three/ four[4] years earlier
England and Wales					
1958–9	21,960	•	•	•	•
1959–60	21,523	•	•	•	•
1960–1	22,528	•	•	•	•
1961–2	24,675	71,114	11,801	3·11	53·7
1962–3	25,865	74,735	12,334	3·08	57·3
1963–4	26,903	79,157	13,581	3·08	60·3
1964–5	29,959	85,375	15,675	3·11	63·5
1965–6	35,260	94,795	17,444	3·10	67·4
1966–7	36,295	103,593	19,519	3·08	72·6
Scotland					
1957–8	3,706	•	•	•	•
1958–9	3,912	•	•	•	•
1959–60	3,783	•	•	•	•
1960–1	4,140	•	•	•	•
1961–2	4,736	15,751	1,456	3·79	39·3
1962–3	5,001	16,994	1,566	3·82	40·0
1963–4	5,438	18,218	1,703	3·74	45·0
1964–5	6,595	21,154	2,024	3·87	48·9
1965–6	7,459	23,241	1,883	3·75	39·8
1966–7	7,383	24,475	2,105	3·56	42·1

Table A.9

Students in Full-time Higher Education, Great Britain

	Universities (including former C.A.T.s)		Colleges of education		Further education		All full-time higher education	
	Actual	Robbins	Actual	Robbins	Actual	Robbins	Actual	Robbins
England and Wales								
1961–2	102,600	•	36,500	•	23,800	•	162,900	•
1962–3	108,700	•	48,400	•	28,000	•	185,100	•
1963–4	116,000	118,900	54,800	52,800	33,300	32,800	204,100	204,500
1964–5	127,200	130,100	62,800	58,900	39,600	35,700	229,700	224,700
1965–6	140,500	143,900	73,300	66,000	47,000	38,100	260,800	248,000
1966–7	154,500	155,400	85,500	71,100	54,500	40,400	294,400	266,900
1967–8	167,600	163,100	94,800	75,200	66,000	42,500	328,300	280,800
Scotland								
1961–2	20,800	•	5,700	•	3,100	•	29,600	•
1962–3	22,000	•	6,300	•	3,100	•	31,400	•
1963–4	23,800	23,500	7,100	6,400	3,100	3,300	34,000	33,200
1964–5	26,300	26,200	7,900	7,000	3,600	3,700	37,800	36,900
1965–6	28,100	29,300	8,900	7,900	4,200	4,300	41,200	41,500
1966–7	29,700	31,500	9,700	8,500	4,700	4,600	44,100	44,600
1967–8	32,100	33,400	10,800	9,000	5,200	4,500	48,100	46,900

Great Britain

1961–2	123,400	.	42,200	.	26,900	.	192,500	.
1962–3	130,700	.	54,700	.	31,100	.	216,500	.
1963–4	139,800	142,400	61,900	59,200	36,400	36,100	238,100	237,700
1964–5	153,500	156,300	70,700	65,900	43,200	39,400	267,500	261,600
1965–6	168,600	173,200	82,200	73,900	51,900	42,400	302,000	289,500
1966–7	184,200	186,900	95,100	79,600	59,200	45,000	338,500	311,500
1967–8	199,700	196,500	105,600	84,200	71,200	47,000	376,400	327,700

Table A.11

Students in Universities and Former
C.A.T.s, Great Britain

	Former colleges of advanced technology	Other universities[5]	Total
1961–2	8,900	114,500	123,400
1962–3	10,300	120,400	130,700
1963–4	11,500	128,300	139,800
1964–5	13,800	139,700	153,500
1965–6	15,800	152,800	168,600
1966–7	17,800	166,400	184,200
1967–8	20,300	179,400	199,700

Table A.12

Current and Capital Grants from Central
Government to Universities, Great Britain

£ million (current prices)

	Current	Capital	Total
Excluding former C.A.T.s			
1961–2	51·5	28·6	80·1
1962–3	60·6	36·5	97·1
1963–4	74·5	43·3	117·8
1964–5	89·6	61·9	151·5
1965–6	106·0	73·3	179·3
1966–7	120·4	70·5	190·9
Including former C.A.T.s			
1966–7	139·5	79·4	218·9

Table A.13
Total Current and Capital
Expenditure in Colleges of
Education, England and
Wales

£ million (current prices)

	Current	Capital	Total
1961–2	17·3	11·6	28·9
1962–3	22·0	13·6	35·6
1963–4	25·9	8·8	34·7
1964–5	31·3	9·9	41·2
1965–6	38·5	10·0	48·5
1966–7	45·9	9·2	55·1

Notes to Appendix A

1. Table A.7
*The numbers of entrants to arts faculties are expressed as a percentage of leavers with arts A levels and similarly for science.

2. Table A.10
Length of course is calculated by subtracting from the undergraduate numbers in year X the number of entrants in years X, X − 1, X − 2, and expressing the remainder as a percentage of entrants in year X − 3 see Robbins Report, Appendix One, p. 153, para. 134.

3. Table A.10
The table excludes the Heriot-Watt College in all years, and includes the former Scottish College of Commerce from 1964–5 onwards.

4. Table A.10
Three years earlier for England and Wales; four years earlier for Scotland.

5. Table A.11
The figures for 'other universities' include in all years Heriot-Watt College (made a university in 1965–6) and the Scottish College of Commerce (incorporated in the University of Strathclyde in 1964–5). In tables excluding C.A.T.s these colleges, as well as the actual C.A.T.s, are excluded, except from 1964–5 onwards when the Scottish College of Commerce has had to be included.

Appendix B
Sources to Tables and Figures

Technical Note

The figures in the tables have been rounded individually. In some cases therefore, the rounded figures in a column or row do not add exactly to the rounded total. The following symbols have been used throughout the tables:

- . = not applicable
- .. = not available
- – = nil or negligible

Abbreviations

In quoting sources in this and the next Appendix, the following abbreviations are used:

U.G.C. Returns: University Grants Committee, *Returns from Universities and University Colleges*, published annually by H.M.S.O., London up to 1965–6. The University Grants Committee's published statistics contain two main sections: a series of large numbered tables and, preceding them, a section of comparative statistics consisting mainly of unnumbered tables. References to tables in the U.G.C. Returns are to the large numbered tables; references to the comparative statistics are simply given as '*U.G.C. Returns*, Summary statistics'.

Stats. Educ.: Statistics of Education, published annually by H.M.S.O., London, for the Department of Education and Science (until April 1964, the Ministry of Education). From 1966–7 these include the *U.G.C. Returns* which are no longer published separately.

RR: Higher Education, Report of the Committee appointed by the Prime Minister under the Chairmanship of Lord Robbins 1961–63, H.M.S.O., London, Cmnd 2154.

RR(One) The Demand for Places in Higher Education, Appendix One to RR.

RR(Two A) and RR(Two B): Students and their Education, Appendixes Two(A) and Two(B) to RR.

RR(Three): Teachers in Higher Education, Appendix Three to RR.

RR(Four): Administrative, Financial and Economic Aspects of Higher Education, Appendix Four to RR.

U.C.C.A.: Universities Central Council on Admissions.

In the book itself, *Higher Education* is referred to as the *Robbins Report* or *Report,* and the Appendixes as *Appendix One,* etc.

Sources

Figure 1

Universities:
    1962–3: *U.G.C. Returns 1962–63,* Table 1, and *Stats. Educ. 1962,* Vol. 2, Table 15(x)
    1967–8: Data supplied by U.G.C.

Note The universities have been grouped as follows:

New universities:	East Anglia, Essex, Kent, Lancaster, Sussex, Warwick, York, Stirling and the Business Schools at London and Manchester
Former C.A.T.s:	Aston, Bath, Bradford, Brunel, City, Loughborough, Salford, Surrey Universities, and Chelsea and the Welsh Colleges
London:	Constituent colleges excluding Chelsea College
Wales:	University of Wales and St David's College, Lampeter
Scotland:	Scottish universities excluding Stirling, but including Heriot Watt and the Scottish College of Commerce

Civic: All English universities, other than Oxford and Cambridge and those listed above

Colleges of
education, and
further education: see sources to Figure 2

Figure 2

(Figures for 1962–3 onwards are in Table 2)
1957–8 to 1961–2: *RR(One)*, p. 164, Table 47
1962–3 to 1967–8: Table A.9

Figures 3 and 4

Table A.1

Figures 5 and 6

Two or more A levels: Table A.1
University entrants (including C.A.T.s):
  Robbins: *RR(One)*, p. 278, Table Z.1 and p. 281, Table Z.4
  Actual:
    1956–1961: *RR(One)*, p. 159, Table 41 and Table T.1
    1962–1967: Table A.8

Table 1

1956: Table A.1, *RR(One)*, p. 159, Table 41 and Table T.1
1961–1967: Tables A.1 and A.8

Table 2

1957–8: *RR(One)*, p. 164, Table 47
1962–3 to 1967–8: Table A.9

Table 3

Entrants:
    1956–1960: *RR(One)*, p. 159, Table 41 and Table T.1
    1961–1967: Table A.8
Age group: *Stats. Educ. 1967*, vol. 2, Table 33(ii)

Note The similar table in the *Robbins Report* (*RR(One)*, p. 148, Table 31) relates entrants to the single age group of eighteen-year-olds in June each year. Table 3 here uses instead of a single age group a mixture of several age groups. The method of calculation is:

$$\text{Entrants as a percentage of the age group} = \frac{\text{Entrants}}{\text{Output of those with one or more A levels}} \times \text{Output of those with one or more A levels as a percentage of the age group}$$

The quantity 'output of those with one or more A levels as a percentage of the age group' relates output to several age groups: the method of calculation is described in *Stats. Educ. 1966*, vol. 2, p. xxi

Table 4

Percentage of the age group obtaining two or more A levels:
  1954: *RR(One)*, p. 112, Table 10
  1961, 1967: Table A.3
Percentage of seventeen-year-olds at school:
  1954: *Stats. Educ. 1962*, Pt. 1, Table 3
  1961, 1967: Table A.4

Table 5

1954–1961 and 1961–1967 Robbins: *RR(One)*, p. 113, Table 11
1961–1967 Actual: Table 4

Note Least squares coefficients from yearly data in *Stats. Educ. 1967*, vol. 1, Table 43, and vol. 2, Table 33(ii)

Figures 7 and 8

Seventeen-year-olds in January:
  1954–1959: Data supplied by Department of Education and Science.
  1960–1967: *Stats. Educ. 1967*, vol. 1, Table 42
Number of seventeen-year-olds at school in January and percentage of seventeen-year-olds at school in January:
  Robbins: *Stats. Educ. 1962*, Pt. 1, Table 3

Actual: *Stats. Educ. 1966*, vol. 1, Table 44 (ii), and *1967*, vol. 1, Table 43 (ii)

Table 6

Stats. Educ. 1966, vol. 2, p. xxiii and *1967*, vol. 2, Table 31

Table 7

Table A.8, and sources to Table A.1

Table 8

U.C.C.A., *Statistical Supplement to Fourth Report, 1965–66*, Table D

Table 9

Stats. Educ. 1962, Pt. 1, Table 31, and *1961* Supplement to Pt. 2, Table 16, and series to *1967*, vol. 2, Tables 24 and 29

Note It has been assumed that the proportions obtaining arts passes and science passes in further education are the same as those in schools.

Figure 9

See sources to Tables 9 and 10

Table 10

Entrants: Table 1. It has been assumed that all entrants to former C.A.T.s before 1965 were to science courses. This assumption does not lead to major error – by 1965 there were only 592 entrants in arts subjects to the former C.A.T.s
School leavers with two or more A levels: Table 9

Table 11

Robbins 1966–7: *RR(One)*, Tables Z.9, Z.12, Z.14
Actual:
   1961–2: *U.G.C. Returns 1961–62*, Table 5, and *RR(One)*,
       Tables Z.9 and Z.14
   1966–7: Data supplied by U.G.C.

Table 12

Home postgraduates: *U.G.C. Returns 1961–62*, Summary Statistics, and series to *Stats. Educ. 1966*, vol. 6, Tables 9 and 10. Data on former C.A.T.s in 1965–6 to 1966–7 from U.G.C. and home postgraduates on courses of teacher training *Stats. Educ. 1967*, vol. 4, Table 1

Students graduating: *U.G.C. Returns 1961–62*, Table 5, and series to *1965–66*, Table 15

Note In years before 1965 the numbers of students shown as graduating underestimate the total number of graduates slightly, owing to the different interpretations put upon the U.G.C.s definition by some universities.

Table 13

U.G.C. Returns 1962–63, Summary Statistics, p. 4 and Table 5, and series. 1966 data supplied by U.G.C.

Notes 1. Up to, and including, the academic year 1964–5, the U.G.C. used an eight group 'faculty' scheme for classifying the subject of study of students in universities. These faculties were: Arts, Social Studies, Pure Science, Applied Science, Medicine, Dentistry, Agriculture and Forestry, Veterinary Science. No precise definition of these groupings was made, only broad examples being given. It was left to the university institution to exercise its discretion in placing the students into the various groups. Thus two institutions offering essentially the same course would not necessarily classify the students on the course in the same way.

Following the recommendations of the Statistical Working Party on the Classification of University Degrees, the U.G.C. adopted for the academic year 1965–6, a new classification scheme for subjects. For details of the new standard subject classification prepared by the Working Party see *Stats. Educ. 1965*, Pt. 2, pp. 177–85. This scheme is an eighty-two point subject-group scheme. Details of the individual points are given in *U.G.C. Returns 1965–66*, Appendix 1. These eighty-two groups were combined in the following manner to obtain a reasonable equivalence with the earlier groupings: Arts: 1–22, 34, 35, 82, $\frac{1}{2} \times 33$, $\frac{1}{4} \times 50$, $\frac{1}{6} \times 65$; Social Studies: 23–32, 68, $\frac{1}{2} \times 33$, $\frac{1}{4} \times 50$, $\frac{1}{6} \times 65$; Pure Science: 36–49, $\frac{1}{2} \times 50$, $\frac{2}{3} \times 65$; Applied Science: 51–64, 66, 67, 74, 75, $\frac{2}{3} \times 65$; Medicine and Dentistry: 76, 77, 78, 81; Veterinary Science: 79, 80.

2. The numbers of postgraduate students on teacher training courses are not collected under the new classification scheme. The numbers of these students were estimated to be 4,000 in 1965–6 and 1966–7.

Table 14

U.G.C. Returns 1957–58, Summary Statistics and Table 1, and series to *Stats. Educ. 1966*, vol. 6, Tables 8, 9, 10 and 11, and data on the former C.A.T.s in 1965–6 from U.G.C.

Table 15

See sources to Figure 2

Table 16

1961: *RR(One)*, p. 123, Table 17
1967: *Report on Entry to Colleges of Education: Autumn 1965/
    Spring 1968*; Central Register and Clearing House Ltd,
    pp. 14, 16

Table 17

Numbers of entrants: Table A.8
Qualifications of entrants:
  Universities: it has been assumed that all entrants have two
  or more A levels. This assumption is reasonably substantiated
  by the Department of Education's School Leavers Survey and
  by data from the U.C.C.A. *Reports* and *Statistical Supple-
  ments*
  Former C.A.T.s:
    1961: *RR(One)*, p. 16, Table 11
    1965–1967: As for other universities
    Intermediate years: By interpolation
  Colleges of education:
    1961–1964: Central Register and Clearing House Ltd
          Reports, see also source to Table 16

1965–1967: Central Register and Clearing House Ltd, *Report on Entry to Colleges of Education, 1965,* and series; see also source to Table 16

Further education: *RR(One)*, p. 16, Table 11. It has been assumed that the spread of qualifications has been constant since 1961. The assumption is arbitrary

Qualified school leavers: *Stats. Educ. 1967,* vol. 2, Table 33(i). Data for school leavers with five or more O levels have been multiplied by 1·032 to allow for passes obtained in further education. It has been assumed that, as in 1961, 92·8 per cent of those with one or more A levels also have five or more O levels in each year.

Note Entrants with O levels but no A levels are expressed as a percentage of output two years earlier.

Table 18

1961–1964: Central Register and Clearing House Ltd *Reports*
1965–1967: Central Register and Clearing House Ltd, *Report on Entry to Colleges of Education, 1965* and series

Figure 10

Table 17

Table 19

Table A.9

Table 20

Stats. Educ. 1967, vol. 3, Table 6

Note The categories used are:
London degrees: First degree, other than Council for National Academic Awards first degrees; higher degrees, including C.N.A.A. higher degrees; post-graduate and research studies
C.N.A.A. degrees and Dip. Tech.:
  1961–2: Dip Tech. students
  1967–8: C.N.A.A. first degrees

National art qualifications: N.D.D., Dip. A.D., A.T.D., A.T.C.
Professional qualifications: Other advanced work.

Table 21

Staff: *U.G.C. Returns 1961–62*, Table 9 and series to *Stats. Educ.
        1966*, vol. 6, Tables 58 and 59. Data for 1967 supplied by
        U.G.C.
Students: see source to Table A.9

Note See text for comments on Categories A, B and C.

Table 22

1938–9 to 1954–5: *RR(Three)*, p. 5, Table 2
1961–2 to 1964–5: *U.G.C. Returns 1961–62,* Tables 5 and 9 and
                  series, and data suppled by U.G.C. on faculty
                  division of staff at Oxford and Cambridge.
1965–6:   *U.G.C. Returns 1965–66*, Tables 7, 8, 19 and
                  data supplied by U.G.C. on faculty division of
                  staff at Oxford, Cambridge and the former
                  C.A.T.s
1966–7:   Data supplied by U.G.C.

Note See Note to Table 13 on subject classification.

Table 23

U.G.C. Returns 1965–66, Tables 22 and 24

Note Expenditure from research grants has been shown separately
from departmental maintenance. Its division into salaries and
other is based on data supplied by the U.G.C.

Table 24

1961–2 to 1965–6: *U.G.C. Returns 1961–62,* Table 12 and series
1966–7:   Data supplied by U.G.C.

Notes 1. Data have been converted to constant prices using
'Report prepared by Professor Tress of the University of Bristol
at the request of the Committee of Vice-Chancellors and
Principals, April 1967'. This has been used on academic salaries
and on the total, other real expenditure being obtained as a
residual.

2. Data excluding former C.A.T.s also exclude throughout the Heriot-Watt College but include the former Scottish College of Commerce for 1964–5 onwards.

3. Data are reduced to exclude capital payments met from income and Selective Employment Tax payments (which are later reimbursed).

Table 25

Expenditure: Table 24
Students: *U.G.C. Returns 1961–62*, Table 4 and series

Notes 1. See notes to Table 24. Student numbers have also been adjusted as specified in Note 2.

2. Two part-time students have been treated as equivalent to one full-time. The number of part-timers on courses of a university standard (in universities excluding C.A.T.s) is reported by the U.G.C. as 1961–2: 18,779; 1962–3: 16,424; 1963–4: 16,528; 1964–5: 18,677; 1965–6: 9,679; 1966–7: 12,811. There was clearly some change of definition in 1965–6 and we have therefore assumed the numbers in that year consistent with earlier years to be 18,000 and likewise in 1966–7.

Table 26

1961–2 to 1965–6: *Stats. Educ. 1966*, vol. 5, Table 8
1966–7: Data supplied by D.E.S.

Notes 1. The figures include the total expenditure of the colleges on revenue account less loan charges and capital expenditure met from revenue.

2. Data have been converted to constant prices by deflating salaries of academic staff and other wages and salaries by the Index of Weekly Wage Rates (*Annual Abstract of Statistics, 1967*, H.M.S.O., Table 154) and other expenditure by the Retail Price Index (ibid, Table 382)

Table 27

Tables 26 and 15

Figures 11 and 12

Tables A.1 and A.2

Table 28

Tables A.1 and A.2

Table 29

See text

Table A.1

Eighteen-year-olds in June:
    Robbins: *RR(One)*, p. 95, Table 1
    Actual:
        1954–1961: *RR(One)*, p. 95, Table 1
        1962–1966: *Annual Abstract of Statistics 1961* to *1967*,
            Table 8
        1967:   *Registrar General's Quarterly Return for England
            and Wales 1967*, 3rd Quarter, H.M.S.O., Appen-
            dix A
Numbers obtaining two or more A levels:
    Robbins: *RR(One)*, Table S.1.
    Actual: *Stats. Educ. 1962*, Pt. 3, Table 18, and series *1967*,
            vol. 2, Table 33
Percentage of the age group getting two or more A levels:
    Robbins: *RR(One)*, p. 112, Table 10
    Actual: see 'Numbers obtaining two or more A levels'

Table A.2

Eighteen-year-olds in June:
    D.E.S. 1966: data supplied by D.E.S., consistent with *Stats.
              Educ. 1966*, vol. 1, Table 43
    Robbins: see sources to Table A.1
Two or more A levels and percentage obtaining two or more A
levels:
    D.E.S. 1966: *Stats. Educ. 1966*, vol. 2, Table 26
    Robbins: see source to Table A.1

Table A.3

Actual: *Stats. Educ. 1967*, vol. 2, Table 33(ii)
Robbins: *RR(One)* pp. 112, 113, Tables 10, 11

Note The total number of those with five or more O levels has been assumed in all years to equal the number of school leavers with five or more O levels multiplied by 1·032.

Table A.4

Actual: *Stats. Educ. 1967*, vol. 1, Table 43(ii)
Robbins: *Stats. Educ. 1962*, Pt.1, Table 3

Table A.5

Children at school: *Stats. Educ. 1962*, Pt. 2, Table 3, and *1967*, vol. 1, Table 43(ii)
A levels: *Stats. Educ. 1967*, vol. 2, Table 33(ii)
G.N.P. at 1958 factor cost: *Annual Abstract of Statistics, 1963*, Table 295, and *1967*, Table 311. The data relate to U.K. but would probably be very similar for England and Wales

Table A.6

Actual: *Stats. Educ. 1961*, Supplement to Pt. 2, Table 15, and *1962*, Pt. 3, Table 16, and series to *1967*, vol. 2, Table 29
Robbins: *RR(One)*, p. 109, Table 7

Table A.7

A level output: *Stats. Educ. 1962*, Pt. 1, Table 31, and Pt. 3, Table 13, and series to *1967*, vol. 2, Tables 24 and 29

Notes 1. Leavers with arts and science A level passes have been divided equally between the two groups.

2. It has been assumed that the proportions obtaining arts passes and science passes in further education are the same as those in schools.

Entrants by faculty: See sources to Table A.8 and Note 1 to Table 13 on faculty definitions

Table A.8

University entrants (including former C.A.T.s):
  1961: *RR(One)*, Table T.1 and p. 159, Table 41

1962–4: University entrants (excluding former C.A.T.s): *Returns 1962–63,* Table 2 and series, and see Note 1 below
Entrants to former C.A.T.s: *Stats. Educ. 1964,* Pt. 2, Table 9, and *Stats. Educ. 1962,* Pt. 2, Table 21, and series; and see Note 2 below

1965: *U.G.C. Returns 1965–66,* Table 2, and see Note 1 below

1966–7: *Stats. Educ. 1966,* vol. 6, Tables 24 and 25 and data supplied by U.G.C.; and see Note 1 below

Colleges of education:

1961: *RR(One),* Table T.1

1962–1967: *Stats. Educ. 1967,* vol. 4, Table 2, and p. xi, and see Notes 3 and 4 below. Provisional data for 1967 was used

Further education:

1961: *RR(One),* p. 159, Table 41

1962–1967: *Stats. Educ. 1965,* Pt. 2, Table 21, and series to *1967,* vol. 3, Table 11; and *Stats. Educ. 1962,* Pt. 2, Table 21, and series to *1967,* vol. 3, Table 15, and see Note 2 below

Notes These notes give the methods used to estimate initial entrants from England and Wales from the number of entrants in the sources above. The methods are those employed by the Committee on Higher Education.

1. *University entrants:* The *U.G.C. Returns,* Table 2, and the comparable tables in *Stats. Educ. 1966* and *1967* cited above show the number of 'full-time graduating and first diploma students entering the institution named for the first time'. These numbers have to be reduced to allow for (a) overseas entrants and entrants from Scotland; (b) those not entering the university sector for the first time.

Until 1964, Table 2 of the *U.G.C. Returns* showed the number of entrants coming from the United Kingdom; in 1965 and after this information was not collected, and it has been assumed that home entrants were the same proportion of all entrants as in 1964. This step was done separately for men and for women entering universities in England and Wales, and in Scotland.

The next step is to reduce the figures of home entrants to

obtain estimates of home initial entrants to the university sector. Because of the definitions used by the U.G.C., the entrants shown in their *Returns* include, in addition to initial entrants to the university sector, entrants taking second first degrees at institutions other than that where they first graduated and medical students who transfer from one institution to another to take their clinical studies. The Committee on Higher Education found in their Undergraduate Survey that 0·9 per cent of home students had taken a degree or diploma at a university before beginning their present course (*RR(One)*, Annex F, p. 200, para. 3). The Committee accordingly reduced the number of home entrants shown by the U.G.C. by 0·9 per cent to allow for non-initial entrants. This has also been done in the present study.

In order to obtain from the number of home initial entrants, estimates of initial entrants from England and Wales only, an allowance has to be made for cross-border traffic between England and Wales, and Scotland. In the Undergraduate Survey, the following pattern was found (*RR(One)*, Annex G):

	Men	Women
Percentage of home entrants to universities in England and Wales coming from Scotland	0·8	0·5
Percentage of home entrants to universities in Scotland coming from England and Wales	22·5	23·6

An analysis of grant-aided students in 1964–5 showed an almost identical pattern, and so it was decided to use the above percentages to deflate the figures of home initial entrants in all years, to obtain estimates of home initial entrants to universities from England and Wales.

An alternative method to the one used here and by the Committee on Higher Education to allow for non-initial entrants is now available due to the revision of some of the U.G.C. questionnaires. This uses information collected separately from the *Return* on (i) medical and dental students who are transferring from one institution to another to embark on the clinical stage of their studies. (These students represent, for example, in 1964–5, some 18 per cent of all medical and dental entrants in the U.G.C. sense); and (ii) on entrants who are classified as entering to begin a course or to continue a course. The results obtained from using this method differ little from the one adopted; the estimates were in fact about 800–900 lower in each year than those used.

2. *Entrants to former C.A.T.s, 1962–1964, and entrants to further education, 1962–1967:* Entrants as such are not collected and published by the Department of Education and Science; the only published data refer to students on the first year of the course. The procedure adopted by the Committee on Higher Education, and followed here, to obtain estimates of initial entrants from England and Wales was as follows:

It was assumed that the proportion of students coming from overseas was the same for first-year students as for all students in each year up to 1964. In 1965 and after, the D.E.S. show the number of first-year overseas students, so that no estimation is necessary. The Committee on Higher Education's Further Education Survey showed that cross-border traffic between England and Wales, and Scotland was negligible (*RR(Two B)*, Table N.3). Thus estimates of first-year students from England and Wales were derived from the numbers of all first-year students. The Further Education Survey also showed that in the C.A.T.s, home initial entrants represented 89·1 per cent of home first-year students in the case of men, and 82·4 per cent in the case of women (*RR(One)*, Table F.8). A similar calculation showed that for further education excluding the C.A.T.s the percentage was 76.9 for men and women. This differs marginally from the figure of 76·1 per cent obtainable from *RR(Two B)* Table N.3. These percentages were used to obtain estimates of initial entrants from England and Wales from the estimates of first-year students from England and Wales.

3. *Entrants to colleges of education:* The figures in the source above refer to students admitted to courses of initial training: these differ from students entering higher education for the first time, particularly because of entrants to postgraduate and one-year specialist training courses. The Committee on Higher Education assumed from their Teacher Training Survey that initial entrants from England and Wales were entrants to colleges in England and Wales on all courses other than post-graduate courses and courses at art training centres and colleges

of education (technical) (*RR(One)*, Annex F). This has been followed here.

4. The 1967 colleges of education figures and total figures include estimates of the number of entrants to colleges of education in January and April 1968.

Table A.9

Universities:
  Robbins: *RR(One)*, p. 169, Table 53
  Actual:
    1961–2: *RR(One)*, p. 164, Table 47
    1962–3 to 1964–5:
      Universities other than C.A.T.s: *U.G.C. Returns 1962–63*, Table 1 and series
      Former C.A.T.s: *Stats. Educ. 1962*, Pt. 2, Table 15(x) and series; and data supplied by Scottish Education Department
    1965–6:   *U.G.C. Returns 1965–66*, Table 3
    1966–7 to 1967–8: *Stats. Educ. 1966*, vol. 6, Tables 8 and 9 and data supplied by U.G.C.
Colleges of education: (Training Colleges & Technical Training Colleges only – i.e. excl. Art Training Centres, University Institutes and Departments of Education):
  Robbins: *RR(One)*, p. 169, Table 53
  Actual:
    1961–2: *RR(One)*, p. 164, Table 47
    1962–3 to 1967–8:
      England and Wales: *Stats. Educ. 1962*, Pt. 2, Table 32 and p. 87, and series to *1966*, vol. 4, Table 1. Provisional data for 1967 was supplied by D.E.S.
      Scotland:
        1962–3 to 1965–6: *Education in Scotland 1964*, H.M.S.O., Table 20, and series
        1966–7 to 1967–8: *Scottish Education Statistics 1967*, H.M.S.O., Table 28, and numbers of overseas students in *Education in Scotland 1966, 1967*

Further education:
  Robbins: *RR(One)*, p. 169, Table 53
  Actual:
    1961–2: *RR(One)*, p. 164, Table 47
    1962–3 to 1967–8:
      England and Wales: *Stats. Educ. 1962*, Pt. 2, Table 15 (x),
                        and series to *1967*, vol. 3, Table 11
      Scotland: data supplied by Scottish Education Department

Table A.10

Home initial entrants: See sources to Table A.8
Home undergraduates and postgraduates: *U.G.C. Returns 1961 –62*, Summary Statistics, and series to *Stats. Educ. 1966*, vol. 6, Tables 8, 9, 10 and 11

Table A.11

See sources to Table A.9

Table A.12

1961–2 to 1965–6: *U.G.C. Returns 1961–62*, Table 13 and series
1966–7: Data supplied by U.G.C.

Note See Note 2 to Table 24.

Table A.13

1961–2 to 1965–6: Table 26 and *Stats. Educ. 1966*, vol. 5, Table 1
1966–7: Data supplied by D.E.S.

Note Capital expenditure excludes that by voluntary bodies.

Appendix C
Sources of Statistics in Text

Page

13   *217,000 to 376,000:* Table 2
    Increase over the preceding twenty-five years: Number of
    students in 1938–9 was 69,000 (*RR*, p. 15, Table 3); increase
    to 1962–3 is thus 148,000

15, 16   *4·5, 6·9, 2·4, 10·9, 4·0 per cent:* Table A.1

18   *80, 65 per cent:* Table 1; *73, 59 per cent: RR(One)*, p. 119,
    Table 14. Strictly, these figures relate to the ratio of univer-
    sity entrants to two or more A level output. As Table 17
    shows, some university entrants have less than two or more
    A levels

20   *£200 million: RR*, p. 202, Table 56

21   *120, 65 per cent: RR(One)*, p. 295, Table Z.15 and p. 258,
    Table S.1

22   *26 per cent:* Table A.1

24   *80, 65, 59 per cent:* Table 1

27   *1 or 2 per cent:* see for example U.C.C.A. *Fifth Report
    1966–7*, Table 5

31   *79,000, 63,000* and *26 per cent:* Table A.1
    Footnote: Stats. Educ. 1966, vol. 2, Table 25

38   *Proportions of leavers who attempted one or more A level
    subjects: Stats. Educ. 1962*, Pt. 3, Table 10, and *1967*, vol. 2,
    Table 19
    A level pass rates: Stats. Educ. 1962, Pt. 3, Tables 4, 6, and
    series to *1967*, vol. 2, Tables 7 and 8

39   *10 per cent: Stats. Educ. 1966*, vol. 2, Tables 6, 8 and 21
    3,800, 7,700: Table A.6
    12, 3, 23, 8 per cent: Stats. Educ. 1967, vol. 2, pp. xx and xxi

41   *172,000, 197,000* and *40 per cent: RR*, p. 260, Table 61

42   *All figures:* see Figure 1

43   *26 per cent:* Table A.1
     21 per cent: Table 28

44   *77 per cent:* The basic source of information on university
     applicants is the scheme run by the Universities Central
     Council on Admissions (U.C.C.A.). There are several draw-
     backs to this as a source however. The first is that in the years
     considered not all university applicants applied through
     U.C.C.A.: details of the coverage of the U.C.C.A. scheme
     are given in the U.C.C.A. annual *Reports*. Another draw-
     back is that the information is collected by a questionnaire
     from the applicants who apply through U.C.C.A., and there
     is some non-response to this inquiry. In order to overcome
     these problems of incomplete cover and of non-response,
     estimates of the number of applicants from England and
     Wales have been made.

     The total number of home applicants reported by
     U.C.C.A. for the years considered here are

	Men	Women	Total		
1963	35,441	16,155	51,596	U.C.C.A. *First Report,*	Table 21
1964	40,800	17,546	58,346	U.C.C.A. *Second Report,*	Table 26
1965	50,566	22,495	73,061	U.C.C.A. *Third Report,*	Table 3

The first step is to exclude those applicants with Scottish
school leaving qualifications. In 1963, U.C.C.A. did not
differentiate between applicants holding S.L.C. or S.C.E.
from those with G.C.E. passes. In 1964, a distinction was
made, and it was found that overall, 4·37 per cent of all
applicants held Scottish qualifications. The number of home
applicants in 1963 and 1964 were thus reduced by this
amount. For applicants in 1965, U.C.C.A. provided data
showing the type of qualification held.

The next stage is to estimate the numbers of A level passes
held by these applicants. This was done using the results
from the U.C.C.A. surveys that are presented in the *Reports*.
For 1965 the information was supplied privately by U.C.C.A.
The distribution of A level passes obtaining amongst the
respondents to the surveys was applied to the total number
of applicants coming from England and Wales in order to

estimate the number of them with two or more A level passes.

In the years we have considered, 1963–5, applicants to Oxford and Cambridge were not included in the U.C.C.A. scheme (unless they had also applied to a university within the U.C.C.A. scheme). The next step therefore, is to estimate the numbers of applicants from England and Wales who apply to Oxford and Cambridge but not to a university within the U.C.C.A. scheme.

Estimates of this group of applicants have been made by assuming that all applicants to Oxford and Cambridge who did not also apply to U.C.C.A. universities are admitted to Oxford or Cambridge. We thus make no allowance for those who only apply to Oxford or to Cambridge and are unsuccessful there. Given this assumption it follows that entrants to Oxford and Cambridge are the sum of non-U.C.C.A. applicants and those who withdraw from the U.C.C.A. scheme to enter Oxford or Cambridge. Provided we can estimate total entrants and U.C.C.A. withdrawals going to Oxford and Cambridge, we can deduce the number of non-U.C.C.A. applicants to Oxford and Cambridge.

Estimates of home initial entrants to Oxford and Cambridge are made in the manner described in Note 1 to Table A.8. The next step is to reduce these to the number of entrants with G.C.E. qualifications. The Robbins Committee's Undergraduate Survey showed that 2 per cent of home undergraduates at Oxford or Cambridge in 1961–2 had Scottish qualifications. The estimates of home initial entrants were thus multiplied by 98 per cent to obtain estimates of initial entrants from England and Wales.

The next part of the calculation is to estimate the numbers of applicants through U.C.C.A. who withdrew from the scheme because they had been accepted at Oxford and Cambridge. Again the problem of non-response to the U.C.C.A. census, and the bias associated with it, arises. It has been assumed that a straight grossing-up of the U.C.C.A. 'sample' results will give a not too inaccurate picture. The U.C.C.A. *Second Report*, Table 12, shows that 36·8 per cent of men and 27·2 per cent of women who withdrew from the

U.C.C.A. scheme for 1964 entered Oxford or Cambridge. Because no similar information is available in the U.C.C.A. *First Report* for 1963, the same percentages were used for 1963. For each year, 1963 and 1964, the percentage of applicants in the 'sample' withdrawing is known, so that estimates of those entering Oxford or Cambridge from the U.C.C.A. scheme can be made. Tabulations on applicants in 1965 who entered Oxford and Cambridge from the U.C.C.A. scheme were provided by U.C.C.A. These figures were then substracted from those of initial entrants to Oxford and Cambridge from England and Wales, to get numbers of applicants to Oxford and Cambridge from England and Wales who did not apply to the U.C.C.A. scheme. 98 per cent of men and 100 per cent of women were assumed to have two or more A levels.

So far we have been discussing the numbers who apply in any one year regardless of whether they have applied in a previous year. But what we want to know is how many of a cohort of school leavers ever apply to university and how many of these ever enter. The best approximation to this that we can aim at is to estimate the total number of initial applicants and of initial entrants in any one year. To convert applicants into initial applicants we assume, for lack of better data, that 85 per cent of men and 90 per cent of women were applying for the first time. This assumption which is based on *RR(One)*, Table U.10 is applied to applicants in all faculties and is highly arbitrary. (This table shows that of applicants who entered universities in 1959, 1960 and 1961, 16 per cent of men and 11 per cent of women had also applied to enter in an earlier year.)

The estimated number of initial applicants with two or more A levels was then expressed as a percentage of the total output of those with two or more A levels: see Table A.1.

Page

45 *14 per cent: Stats. Educ. 1966,* vol. 2, Table 19
47 *37 per cent: U.G.C. Returns 1961–62,* Table 5, and data supplied by U.G.C.
   43 per cent: Table 11

51 *30,000: RR*, pp. 154–5, paras. 475–7
Footnote: U.C.C.A., *Third Report, Statistical Supplement, 1964–5,* Table G

53 *20, 30 per cent: RR*, p. 104, para. 301

54 *8, 11 per cent:* Table A.10
13·2, 14·4, 29 per cent: U.G.C. Returns, Summary Statistics, and *Stats. Educ. 1966,* vol. 6, Tables 8 and 9

56 *30 per cent:* Data supplied by U.G.C.
24 per cent: RR(Two A), p. 49, Table 44
Note 7: 97 per cent: Data supplied by U.G.C.
55, 51, 32, 28, 12 per cent: Data supplied by U.G.C.
Applied science here includes agriculture and forestry, and medicine includes dentistry and veterinary science
4, 9 percentage points: comparison with 1961–2 figures given in *RR(Two A),* p. 49, Table 44

57 *70 per cent: RR(Two A),* p. 254, Table 6
£10 million: RR, p. 67

59 *One third, two thirds, a fifth:* The number of overseas postgraduates is given in *Stats. Educ. 1966,* vol. 6, Table 9. However, this source does not give the faculty/subject group distribution of these students, Information on this distribution is given in *Commonwealth Universities Yearbook 1968,* London: Association of Commonwealth Universities, 1968, Appendix IV, which shows the following numbers of overseas postgraduates in universities in the United Kingdom: Humanities 1,651; Education 562; Social Studies 1,894; Pure Science 1,842; Applied Science 1,989; Medicine Dentistry and Health 997; Agriculture, Forestry and Veterinary Science 317; a total of 9,252. The *U.G.C. Returns* show a corresponding total of 9,151, and so numbers were grossed down to this total. The definitions used by the A.C.U. are not exactly the same as those used by the U.G.C.: but this probably does not lead to major errors. For a note on the difference, in terms of coverage of institutions and dates of collection, between the data from these two sources, see *RR(Two A),* Annexes D and S.

60 *500: Stats. Educ. 1966,* vol. 4, p. xi, and *Education in Scotland, 1966,* p. 73
7,060: Stats. Educ. 1966, vol. 3, Table 14(i)

675: Stats. Educ. 1962, Pt. 2, p. 87, and *Education in Scotland, 1962*, Table 22

4,540: Stats. Educ. 1962, Pt. 2, Table 21

16·2, 13·0 per cent: For all students in advanced full-time further education in England and Wales, see Table 19

61   *60, 53 per cent:* Table 2 ·

65   *80,000 and note: 82,000: RR*, p. 259, para. 814

111,000: RR, p. 157, para. 482

70   *85, 95 per cent:* Home students are taken from: *Stats. Educ. 1962*, Pt. 2, Table 32, and series to *1966*, vol. 4, Table 1. Provisional data for 1967 was supplied by D.E.S.

Home entrants as in Table A.8

71   *More than a million:* In 1967 there were in total 3·2 million students enrolled. Only 1·1 million of these were taking courses leading to recognized qualifications. Many of the other students were doing recreational courses in evening institutes. The total number of students in evening institutes was 1·4 million. *Stats. Educ. 1967*, vol. 3, Table 1

74   *30 with 2,000 full-timers each:* see p. 64

79   *7·4, 6·9, 6·8, 7·8, 8·5, 6·6, 7·0: U.G.C. Returns 1962–63*, Tables 1 and 9, and series to *Stats. Educ. 1966*, vol. 6, Tables 8, 9, 10, 11, 58 and 59

10·1, 11·1, 10·5: Full-time students: Table 15; staff: *Stats. Educ. 1961*, Pt. 2, Table 29, and series to *1967*, vol. 4, Table 1

3,600: Stats. Educ. 1961, Pt. 2, Table 29

9,100: Stats. Educ. 1967, vol. 4, Table 1

86   *0·30, 0·49, 0·55 per cent:* Expenditure: Table 24; G.N.P.: *National Income and Expenditure 1968*, H.M.S.O., 1968, Table 1. The data relate to U.K. and the percentages quoted may overstate the percentage of British G.N.P. devoted to higher education by 2–3 per cent

70, 74 per cent: Tables 24 and A.12

£140 million: England and Wales: *Stats. Educ. 1966*, vol. 5, Table 28. Scotland: *Scottish Educational Statistics, 1967*, Table 49. Figures relate to value of projects completed in the year

0·78 per cent: Table A.12 and *National Income and Expenditure 1968*, op. cit., Table 1

87 *32, 55 per cent:* H.M. Treasury, *A Selection of Unit Costs in Public Expenditure*, H.M.S.O., 1968, p. 11, Table 9
   Note 18: D.E.S.
90 *25,000:* see *Hansard*, 27 October 1967, cols. 591–2
   60,000: Table 2
   Note 1: 200,000: Table 2
   220,000–225,000: Hansard, 27 October 1967
95 *43,000: RR (One)*, p. 167, Table 51
   66,000: Table A.9
   20,000: Table A.9
   100,000: In the past the number of home students in colleges of education in year (X) has been approximately equal to the number of home initial entrants in years (X) and (X–1) plus 90 per cent of entrants in year (X–2)

Appendix D
Glossary

What follows is an ordered explanation of the main technical terms used in this book. In general the definitions are the same as in the *Robbins Report*. To look up a particular term the reader should turn first to the index at the end of this glossary. This is in alphabetical order and shows the paragraph in the glossary where the particular term is explained.

1   *Sectors of post-school education* covered in the study

1.1   *Universities.* From 1965–6, the universities included the former colleges of advanced technology and the former Heriot-Watt College in Scotland. From 1964–5 they included the former Scottish College of Commerce which was incorporated in that year in the University of Strathclyde. However, in this book we include these institutions in the universities throughout, except when otherwise stated. Where we present figures 'excluding former C.A.T.s' all the above institutions are excluded, except the Scottish College of Commerce from 1964–5 onwards.

1.2   *Colleges of education* are colleges for educating future teachers. They exclude university departments of education and the central activity of university institutes (or schools) of education. They include general, specialist and technical training colleges but exclude art training centres. Before 1963, the colleges of education in England and Wales were called teacher training colleges.

1.3   *Further education* comprises all other full-time post-school education leading to advanced qualifications provided in institutions maintained by (local) education authorities or receiving direct grants from central government, e.g. polytechnics, technical colleges, Art colleges, colleges of commerce and central institutions.

2 *Levels of post-school education*

2.1 University students are divided into undergraduates and postgraduates. *Undergraduates* are those reading for first degrees and first diplomas. *Postgraduates* are defined as those taking courses for which a first degree or approximately equivalent qualification is a condition of entry (excluding 'occasional' students). All the university students described above are classified as in *higher education*. 'Occasional' students and those classified in the University Grants Committee *Returns* as taking courses 'not of a university standard' are excluded.

2.2 Students in colleges of education work for the *Teachers Certificate* or for a combined degree and certificate, and are classified as in *higher education*.

2.3 Students in *further education* may be engaged on *advanced courses* or non-advanced courses or on courses not leading to any recognized qualification. Only advanced courses are classified as *higher education*. In England and Wales, they are defined as those above the standard required for the Advanced level of the General Certificate of Education or the Ordinary National Certificate. A detailed list of such courses may be found in *RR(One)*, Part I, Section 2 and Annex D. In Scotland, advanced courses are those above the standard required for the Higher grade of the Scottish Certificate of Education; advanced students being subdivided into Category I (which excludes most students taking the first year of advanced courses) and others.

3 *Methods of study*

Full-time courses only are covered. These are those involving full-time study through the week. In universities and colleges of education, full-time students exclude those whose courses last less than an academic year, who are classified as part-time. In further education in England and Wales all students are included who, on the particular day of the year to which the returns relate, were taking full-time courses of whatever length. Full-time courses are divided into continuous courses and sandwich courses, in which the period of full-time study in college is broken by a period (or periods) of industrial training forming an integral part of the course.

4   *Subjects of study*

The basic subject divisions that have been used are:

Humanities ⎫
Education   ⎬ Arts subjects
Social studies ⎭
Pure science ⎫
Applied science ⎬ Science subjects
Agriculture ⎪
Medicine   ⎭

Medicine includes dentistry and veterinary sciences, unless otherwise stated.

5   *Qualified school leavers and entry rates*

5.1   The term *qualified school leavers* refers to the numbers obtaining each level of school leaving qualification (for example, two A level passes in the General Certificate of Education, one A level pass, five or more O level passes but no A level passes) that at present satisfy entry requirements for each form of higher education. The term includes those who obtain their qualifications after leaving school.

5.2   The *entry rates* to higher education are the proportions of 'school leavers' with each level of qualification who enter.

5.3   A particular entry rate is equal to the *application rate* (the proportion of qualified school leavers who apply) multiplied by the *acceptance rate* (the proportion of qualified applicants who enter). There is a different entry rate for school leavers with each level of qualification. But for convenience the entry rates are sometimes referred to collectively as the entry rate, and the proportions of qualified school leavers who enter are also referred to in the singular.

6   *Other terms*

6.1   The concept of the *age group* is best illustrated by reference to those entering higher education. The entrants in any year are of various ages. Those of each age entering are expressed as a percentage of their own age group, and these separate percentages are then summed. This gives a percentage of a composite age group, suitably weighted to allow for the numbers of each age entering and the size of the age groups from which they come. Where the data did not permit this type of calculation, an approximation has been used: all entrants have been expressed as a percentage of the single age group from which the largest number of entrants was thought to be drawn.

6.2 *Home students* are those ordinarily resident in the United Kingdom apart from their period as students. Other students are *overseas students*.

6.3 *Initial entrants* to higher education are those entering higher education as a whole for the first time.

Index to Glossary

List of Tables

Appendix A

List of Figures

All Their Future

Ronald G. Cave

The raising of the school leaving age has again been postponed.
But the problem of what sort of education is most relevant for the
non-academic fourteen- to fifteen-year-old remains. He is
maturing younger, spending harder and criticizing more deeply
society's values. He is, to all intents and purposes, an adult, and
any educational programme which fails to take this into account
is ethically dubious and strategically downright foolish.

All Their Future examines the exciting new curricula and teaching
methods which are being developed in this area. The author argues
strongly that a curriculum must be evaluated by its relevance both
to the concerns of the individual and society, that it should figure
personal relationships prominently, and that the young adult deserves
to be a partner in his own education.

A Penguin Education Special

The Hornsey Affair

Staff and Students, of Hornsey College of Art

On 28 May 1968, the students and some members of the staff of Hornsey College of Art, North London, took control of their college. It was the first step in a brave, inspiring, but short-lived experiment in communal education.

Here, for the first time, is the full story of the Hornsey affair – its causes and results, its moments of tragedy and humour, its final betrayal – written by those members of the college who were most deeply involved. It is not a comfortable story. It is idealistic, angry, partisan and on occasions, perhaps, even naïve. But it is the authentic voice of a growing body of young people who believe their education should be relevant *and* joyous; who cannot accept that it or they should be insulated from the problems of the contemporary world; and who are rightly contemptuous of a system whose chief spokesman sees the function of education as 'gorging at the vocational trough'.

These are the Hornsey Students and this is their manifesto. For six weeks they reasserted in practice the age-old ideal of the university as a community of learning. That this assertion had to be achieved by a revolutionary act is a bitter comment on our current attitudes towards education; that it was crushed in the way it was is tragic.

A Penguin Education Special

The New Polytechnics: The People's Universities

Eric Robinson

Challenged from below by an increasing tide of student unrest, harrassed from above by economic pressures, the universities – amongst the last strongholds of élitist education – seem unlikely to survive in their present form for very much longer.

'Sooner or later,' writes Eric Robinson, 'this country must face a comprehensive reform of education beyond school – a reform which will bring higher education out of the ivory towers and make it available for all.'

The author traces the developments in higher education since the war, and argues that the divisions between university and technical college are indefensible on economic, social and educational grounds. The new polytechnics which the Department of Education and Science are proposing to establish could, by bringing together academic, vocational, full- and part-time students, become higher education's equivalent of the comprehensive school.

A Penguin Education Special